LORENZO IN SEARCH OF THE SUN

LORENZO
IN SEARCH OF
THE SUN

D. H. Lawrence in Italy, Mexico and the American Southwest

BY ELIOT FAY

Bookman Associates, Inc.
New York

FOR

ROBERT AND HELEN

CONTENTS

INTRODUCTION

ONE may like D. H. Lawrence or one may dislike him, but one can no longer ignore him. Since the last war the tide of interest in this highly controversial writer has risen steadily, as witnessed by the many new editions of his works and by the various biographical or critical studies that have been devoted to him. Some who became acquainted with Lawrence twenty years ago are now rereading him, while others who are reading him now for the first time are experiencing the delightful shock of discovery.

T. S. Eliot has said that Lawrence was "a Johnson surrounded by a shoal of Boswells." And William Tindall remarked, in *D. H. Lawrence and Susan His Cow:* "The growing body of primary material . . . which has appeared since his death has given us more information about Lawrence than about any of his contemporaries, and has made him both a suitable subject for further investigation and a splendid center from which to set out on a study of his times."

During the last two or three years Tindall's advice has been taken by such writers as Richard Aldington, Harry T. Moore, Father Tiverton, Witter Bynner, and Anthony West. Aldington and Bynner had the advantage of knowing Lawrence personally. Each of the five achieved, within certain

9

self-imposed limits, an excellent piece of work. But in my opinion none has equalled Piero Nardi's *Vita di D. H. Lawrence*, published in Milan in 1947. Nardi's is a complete, objective, and beautifully balanced book.

I wonder if the reader would be bored with the story, briefly told, of my own interest in the D. H. Lawrence legend. I think that I shall risk it. It all began about fifteen years ago, when I spent a couple of summers in Taos, New Mexico. Like any other Easterner, I was excited by the plaza with its *portales,* the Indian pueblo with its *kivas,* and the Mexican village of Ranchos with its Penitente church. I admired the Sangre de Cristo Range, and the Sacred Mountain rising in purple majesty against the evening sky. I inhaled with delight the smoke of the burning *piñón* wood that ascended at meal time from hundreds of little adobe houses all over Taos Valley.

To be sure, I had read some of Lawrence's novels, poems, and essays. But I had no idea that he had ever been in the United States, not to mention Taos. One day while I was wandering through the gallery of the local art association, I came across a shelf of books by Taos people. Three of them were concerned with D. H. Lawrence. They were: Frieda Lawrence's *Not I, But the Wind,* Mabel Dodge Luhan's *Lorenzo in Taos,* and Dorothy Brett's *Lawrence and Brett.*

I read these books one after another, with the greatest eagerness. In them I learned how Lawrence had been called from Sicily to Taos by Mabel Dodge Luhan; how tensions had developed between Mabel and Frieda Lawrence, and later between Frieda and Dorothy Brett; how Lawrence had on two occasions spent considerable time in Mexico; and how he had, in the end, gone back to the shores of the Mediterranean that he loved so much.

There were many people in Taos who had known Lawrence when he had come there ten years earlier. Mabel Dodge Luhan herself still occupied the charming house where she and Tony, her Indian husband, had entertained him. In the village one was likely enough to see Frieda Lawrence or Dorothy Brett. "Spud" Johnson, whom Lawrence had called "the Spoodle," was in his office editing *The Taos Valley News*. And the poet Witter Bynner, Johnson's friend, was only sixty miles off in Santa Fe.

Some of these interesting folk I met, others I did not. I have never believed in badgering people because they had known a famous person, or even because they themselves were famous. Moreover I hardly suspected at the time that I would ever study D. H. Lawrence seriously, or write anything about him for publication. At the end of my second summer in Taos I said goodbye to that enchanted country, and have never gone back there since.

Of course, the accounts by Frieda Lawrence, Mabel Dodge Luhan and Dorothy Brett would be for any student of Lawrence, as they were for me, merely a point of departure from which to set forth on a voyage of further investigation. After one's curiosity has been aroused by personal narratives like these, one reads the books by Lawrence that one has missed, and reads again a number of those that he has read before. Then, eager to know much more about the extraordinary man behind these most unusual books, he retires to his study with such primary sources of information as the works of Ada Lawrence, "E. T.," Catherine Carswell, Middleton Murry, Earl and Achsah Brewster, Knud Merrild, Richard Aldington, and Witter Bynner. Somewhere along the line he becomes absorbed in Lawrence's *Letters*, splendidly edited with a penetrating introduction by Aldous Huxley.

Huxley expresses considerable impatience with the women

11

who have written about D. H. Lawrence. They have seen themselves, he says, "in the part of mother, of lover, or . . . of 'holy woman.' They write as though they had invented and patented Lawrence; as though they had composed him, copyrighted him and deposited him in the British Museum and the Library of Congress; as though no D. H. Lawrence were genuine without their signature upon the bottle." He is even more exasperated with Middleton Murry, by whom he believes Lawrence to have been "victimized."

Aldous Huxley's opinions have been echoed recently by Anthony West, who writes: "Lawrence, in the books of E. T., of Murry, Brett, Luhan and Carswell, is like the charm in the folktale, that must be sold for a lower price each time it changes hands, till it comes to be worth a grain of sand, a dead leaf, nothing." This is nonsense, of course. The books that West enumerates are, to be sure, of unequal value. But each one throws its own peculiar light on some moment in the life of Lawrence, or on some aspect of his personality. To know him well it is necessary to read them all.

In this small volume I have endeavored to interpret, as I see them, the main currents in the life of D. H. Lawrence from 1920 to 1930. I chose this particular segment of his life because it seems to me that it has incomparable dramatic power. During these years "Lorenzo," as Frieda and others often called him, was lured from Italy to Mexico, and from Mexico back to Italy again. Simultaneously he strayed from a charmed circle, shared only with his wife, into the danger zone of the influence of other women, then from this danger zone back once more to the charmed circle. And finally, having been touched by the shadow of death, he fought against death with all the courage at his command, only to realize in the end that true courage, now, consisted in acceptance.

Through all these conflicts Lawrence, instinctive artist

that he was, wrote steadily. These years from 1920 to 1930 witnessed the composition of such important yet dissimilar works as *Sea and Sardinia, Birds, Beasts and Flowers, The Plumed Serpent, Mornings in Mexico, Lady Chatterley's Lover,* and *Etruscan Places.* Meanwhile he was living for the most part in lands of southern sunshine—in lands where men still speak the musical Latin tongues. It was then, as H. T. Moore remarks, that "he produced some of his most brilliant work," whose surface "flows with rich tropical colors as he travels back and forth across the warm belts of the earth."

No book has yet been written, so far as I know, which covers Lawrence's life from 1920 to 1930 in a completely satisfying way. You must go to one set of sources for the truth about his stay in Taormina, to another set for the facts concerning his first visit to Taos, to still another for the details of his sojourn in Chapala, and so on. However this brief study is considerably more than a *pastiche* composed of borrowings from the various writers, male and female, who knew Lawrence here or knew him there. In many instances it has been necessary to compare the stories of several different individuals recounting a certain episode in several different ways. Lawrence's first visit to Taos, for example, is not handled in the same way by Frieda Lawrence as it is by Mabel Dodge Luhan or Knud Merrild. His second visit there is one thing as seen by Frieda and another thing as seen by Mabel or by Dorothy Brett. I have had to seek for evidence, internal or external, to explain conflicting statements and, above all, to establish a fairly reliable chronology of events. The chapters on Chapala and on Oaxaca, as well as those on Taos, were strengthened by personal investigation in the field.

I wish to thank the authors and publishers of all the books from which I have quoted or to which I have referred, and especially the Honourable Dorothy Brett, the Viking Press, Alfred A. Knopf, Inc., and Harcourt, Brace and Co., who generously gave me their permission to make frequent and occasionally lengthy quotations from Dorothy Brett's *Lawrence and Brett* (Lippincott), Aldous Huxley's edition of Lawrence's *Letters* (Viking), Frieda Lawrence's *Not I, But the Wind* (Viking), Mabel Dodge Luhan's *Lorenzo in Taos* (Knopf), Catherine Carswell's *The Savage Pilgrimage* (Harcourt, Brace), and from the other works, listed in the Bibliography, in which they hold the copyright.

This project was made possible in part through a grant-in-aid allocated by the Research Committee of Emory University from funds made available jointly by the Carnegie Foundation and the University. Neither the Foundation nor the University is in any way responsible for the opinions I have expressed. On the other hand, I am deeply grateful to both for their liberal help.

I am grateful also to the late G. R. G. Conway, of Mexico City and Cuernavaca, who knew Lawrence well and who placed at my disposal his fine collection of Lawrenciana. His library assistant, Señorita Elisa Vargas Lugo, made me feel at home in Mexico as I have rarely felt at home in any other foreign country. I cannot omit a hearty *Salud* to that kindly man and excellent artist, Emil Holzhauer, who was my companion in Mañana Land for several unforgettable months. And in closing I want to thank my colleague, Professor H. Blair Rouse, for his patient and discerning criticism.

E. F.

Cuernavaca

TAORMINA

Most of my readers will, I think, be familiar already with the principal events in D. H. Lawrence's life. For those who are not, and for those who would like to review them before proceeding to a study of the years from 1920 to 1930, I am going to present the following very brief outline of the life of Lawrence up to the age of thirty-five. David Herbert Lawrence was born in Eastwood, Nottinghamshire, in 1885. His father was a burly and genial coal-miner, his mother a woman of intelligence and imagination. There were four other children—two boys and two girls. When David was thirteen he won a scholarship which enabled him to enter the Nottingham High School. After his graduation he remained for a time in Nottingham, where he was employed at thirteen shillings a week by a manufacturer of surgical supplies. When a pulmonary disorder compelled him to abandon this occupation, he returned to Eastwood as a pupil teacher in the British School there. He had already fallen in love with Jessie Chambers, the girl to whom in Sons and Lovers he refers as "Miriam." Lawrence taught in Eastwood for a couple of years and then began to study for his teaching certificate at Nottingham University College. On obtaining the certificate he was given a position at the

15

Davidson Road School in Croydon. His first poems were published in *The English Review* in 1909. The following year his mother, to whom he was so passionately attached, died of cancer. Before her death she was able to see an advance copy of her son's first published novel, *The White Peacock*. The acceptance of this novel induced Lawrence to resign his teaching position and thenceforth to earn his living with his pen. *Sons and Lovers*, undoubtedly his best known book, appeared in 1913. In 1914, after a period of travel in Germany and Italy, Lawrence married Frieda von Richthofen, daughter of a German baron and cousin of a German ace who shot down eighty Allied planes in World War I. Frieda was also the divorced wife of an English university professor, by whom she had had a son and two daughters. She was six years older than Lawrence. During the war, while the Lawrences were living in Cornwall, the fact that Frieda was German brought upon them a certain amount of persecution. Immediately after the war Frieda left England to visit her family. Lawrence, unwilling to go to Germany so soon after the Armistice, and feeling the need of southern sunshine, set out for Italy. He was aided in his venture by a legacy of twenty pounds from Rupert Brooke.

*   *   *

On his arrival in Florence in November, 1919, Lawrence was met by Norman Douglas, the author of *South Wind,* and by Maurice Magnus, who pretended to be a grandson of Emperor Wilhelm I of Germany, and for whose *Memoirs of the Foreign Legion* he was to write an extraordinary introduction. In the first paragraph of this introduction Lawrence tells us that he landed in Italy with only nine pounds in his pocket and with only twelve pounds more in his London bank. Frieda, when she arrived in Florence, might possibly be able to contribute two or three additional pounds.

If they were going to spend the winter in Italy they would have to plan their budget with considerable care. Douglas and Magnus had taken a room for Lawrence at the Pension Balestri, where they themselves were staying. From there he wrote to Catherine Carswell: "Am here in the rain, waiting for Frieda, of whom I hear nothing yet. Italy is rather spoiled by the war—a different temper, not so nice a humour by far."

It was at this time that Rebecca West and two of her friends dropped in to call on Lawrence. In the little book about him that she published eleven years later, after his death, she writes: "He was staying in a poorish hotel overlooking . . . the Arno. . . . His room was one of the cheaper ones at the back. . . . It was a small, mean room in which he sat tapping away at a typewriter." Then she goes on to describe her meeting with him:

He was one of the most polite people I have ever met, in both naive and subtle ways. . . . He made friends as a child might do, by shyly handing me funny little boxes he had brought from some strange place he had recently visited; and he made friends too as if he were a wise old philosopher at the end of his days, by taking notice of one's personality, showing that he recognized its quality, and giving it his blessing.

Finally she records her impressions of his physical appearance and of his movements:

His skin, though he had lived so much in southern countries, was very white, his eyes were light, his hair and beard were a pale luminous red. His body was very thin, and because of the flimsiness of his build it seemed as if a groove ran down the centre of his chest and his spine, so that his shoulder-blades stood out in a pair of almost wing-like projections. He moved quickly and joyously.

The next day Rebecca West and Norman Douglas went walking with Lawrence through the Tuscan countryside.

17

She was never to see him face to face again. But she was to remain in touch with him by correspondence, and when he died she was to become one of the champions of his life and of his work.

Frieda finally reached Florence one morning at four o'clock. Lawrence immediately took her for a drive in an open carriage. She was enchanted, as she writes in *Not I, But the Wind,* by "the pale, crouching Duomo," the Giotto tower whose top was shrouded in moonmist, Michelangelo's "David," and the Ponte Vecchio. Florence seemed to her to be indeed "the lily town, delicate and flowery." In the days that followed, Frieda enjoyed conversing in German with Norman Douglas and thought the discussions between him and Lawrence extremely witty. She appreciated the hospitality of the English colony in Florence, yet sensed corruption there.

Lawrence and Frieda soon left Florence for a very brief visit in Rome. Here they had the unpleasant experience of being evicted from their pension because Frieda was German. And after they had found hospitality with an English family, Lawrence was further embarrassed by the loss of ten pounds that he had just changed into Italian currency. They decided to try the mountain village of Picinisco. It was beautiful, but so cold they couldn't bear it. So they left the place at half-past five one morning, walked five miles to the nearest town, rode in a bus to Caserta, took a train to Naples, and there, at last, caught the Capri steamer.

At Capri, in December, the Lawrences rented the top floor of the ancient Palazzo Ferraro, from which they could look out over the bay of Naples to the island of Ischia. Their kitchen had to be shared with a Socialist from Rumania. The Rumanian pointed out to them the writer

Compton Mackenzie, whom he admired tremendously. Of Mackenzie, Lawrence wrote to Catherine Carswell:

We lunch or dine sometimes with ——————— —————,
and he is nice. But one feels the generations of actors behind
him and can't be quite serious. . . . He seems quite rich, and does
himself well, . . . walking in a pale blue suit to match his eyes,
and a woman's large brown velour hat to match his hair.

At Christmas time Lawrence received from the American
poet Amy Lowell, who admired him, an unexpected gift
of twenty pounds. Immediately he sent five pounds to
Magnus, who was always in financial difficulties and who
wanted to go and stay for a time at the monastery of Monte
Cassino. Magnus, writing from Monte Cassino to express
his gratitude, begged Lawrence to visit him at the monastery. In February, 1920, Lawrence did so, taking the pre-
caution, however, of leaving his checkbook at home. When,
having reached the mountain-top, he looked down upon
the distant plain, it seemed to him that it represented the
world of the present, which he despised because of its
mechanization and venality. Monte Cassino, on the other
hand, symbolized the peaceful world of bygone days, into
which a tormented individual might escape. Lawrence,
although he longed for peace, refused to run away from
the problems that beset mankind today. He preferred, as he
explained to Magnus, to put the monastery of Monte Cassino behind him and to go down again to the plain, there
to wrestle with his destiny as best he might.

Magnus himself disgusted Lawrence. Because the monastery was cold, he lent his guest a very expensive overcoat
in which he obviously took considerable pride. Before each
altar in the church Magnus knelt down with a fervor that
seemed positively histrionic. Lawrence noticed that the

19

monks appeared to look askance at Magnus. But before he left the monastery he obliged his host by reading the record of the latter's experiences in the French Foreign Legion, and by writing to recommend the manuscript to some London publishers.

Lawrence seems to have liked Capri pretty well for a time. Tiring of it at last, however, he wrote to Lady Cynthia Asquith: "Capri . . . is a gossipy, villa-stricken, two-humped chunk of limestone." He declared that Amalfi was much more beautiful. But it was to Sicily, before the end of February, that he decided to go.

In Taormina Lawrence took Fontana Vecchia, a roomy villa with spacious grounds around it. He rented it for a year, at a cost of only twenty-five pounds. The place proved so delightful that he later renewed his lease for a second year. In March, he wrote to Mrs. R. P.:

I feel at last we are settled down and can breathe. . . . We've got a nice big house, with fine rooms and a handy kitchen, set in a big garden, mostly vegetables, green with almond trees, on a steep slope at some distance above the sea. . . . To the left, the coast of Calabria and the Straits of Messina. It is beautiful, and green, green, and full of flowers. . . . There are a good many English people, but fewer than Capri, . . . and one needn't know them. . . . Etna is a beautiful mountain, far lovelier than Vesuvius. . . .

Frieda was delighted with Fontana Vecchia. The grounds were covered with orange and lemon trees. "Along our rocky road," she writes, "the peasants rode past into the hills on their donkeys, singing loudly; the shepherds drove their goats along, playing their reed pipes as in the days of the Greeks." In Taormina she felt the influence of many civilizations: "Greek and Moorish and Norman and beyond into the dim past." The shopping was done by their servant, Grazia, and Frieda loved to watch the old crone slyly trying to "rook" Lawrence out of a few *lire*. All through the winter roses bloomed. Their daily lives were governed by a simple rhythm, Lawrence helping, as he always had, with the household tasks. Frieda made "cakes and tarts, big and little, sweet pies and meat pies, and put them on the sideboard in the dining room and called them Mrs. Beeton's show."

Early in April the Lawrences left Taormina with some friends to spend a few days in Siracusa. From the windows of their train, they saw that purple anemones were blooming in the fields and that the corn was green, though Mount Etna still wore her crown of snow. As they gazed at the blue Mediterranean, they half expected to see the ship of Odysseus plowing through the waves. In the harbor of Siracusa there were fishing-boats with painted eyes upon their bows, and in the streets there were carts upon whose sides were painted legendary scenes. Lawrence exulted in all this beauty. But what a joy it was thought Frieda, to return to Fontana Vecchia, to "our own house above the almond trees, and the sea in the cove below," the lovely dawn-sea, "where the sun rose with a splendour like trumpets every morning!"

Just as the Lawrences were beginning to feel at peace with the world, Magnus arrived in Taormina. He had left Monte Cassino because of difficulties with the police, and wanted Lawrence to return to the monastery to retrieve his personal belongings. Lawrence refused to do this, but gave the man a hundred *lire*. When he remonstrated with Magnus for putting up at the most expensive hotel in Taormina, the latter took lodgings in the house of a Sicilian named Melenga. Magnus left for Malta without paying Melenga, and it was Lawrence who settled his account. A little later the Lawrences also took an excursion to Malta. At Siracusa, however, a strike delayed them; and whom should they

21

meet but Magnus, also stranded in Siracusa, and desperately anxious for Lawrence to pay his hotel bill there. Lawrence obliged again. As soon as the strike was over he and Frieda took second-class passage on a steamer bound for Malta. Imagine their amazement when, glancing up at the first-class deck, they saw Magnus standing there with a big cigar in his mouth, chatting with one of the officers! When they left the ship at Malta he favored them with a condescending nod. Six months later they were delivered forever from Magnus' importunities, for his affairs became so complicated that he committed suicide.

By the twenty-eighth of May the Lawrences were back again in Taormina. The summer heat was trying, but Lawrence solved this problem by lounging about barefooted, in pajamas. One very hot day he went to the outdoor trough for a drink of water. There, slithering down from its hole in the garden wall, was a yellow snake. As he stood with his pitcher in his hand, the snake began to drink from the trough. After a few sips it lifted its head to look at him, then drank again. Because he knew that the snake was poisonous, he felt afraid. In order to overcome his fear he seized a log, waited until the snake had started back to its hole, and then hurled the missile at it with all his might. But his aim was bad, and in an instant the snake had disappeared. Now Lawrence felt ashamed. He was very sorry he had tried to kill this creature, which, though venomous, was beautiful, and therefore entitled to his hospitality. All this he tells in "Snake," one of the most remarkable poems in *Birds, Beasts and Flowers*. The latter was a poetical collection which he had promised to his agent Curtis Brown, and which he was to finish in New Mexico in 1923. This collection belongs to the group of "unrhyming poems" which he began to write after his marriage and which he

22

continued up to the time of his death. Kenneth Rexroth, in his introduction to Lawrence's *Selected Poems*, states that they represent "the mature Lawrence, in complete control of his medium, or completely controlled by his demon. He never has any trouble. He can say exactly what he wants to say. Except for the death poems, he would never write better."

In August Frieda went by herself to Baden-Baden, while Lawrence spent a fortnight in Florence. There he wrote *Tortoises*, a suite of poems which was eventually incorporated in *Birds, Beasts and Flowers*. After completing the *Tortoise* poems, Lawrence went on to Venice, where Frieda joined him. In October they both returned to Taormina. Here it rained so hard and so long that Lawrence remained indoors for weeks on end, painting and reading up in Italian history. In November Martin Secker published his fifth and sixth novels, *Women in Love* and *The Lost Girl*, the latter with its *dénouement* in Italy.

The heroine of *The Lost Girl*, Alvina, lives in an English mining town. At thirty she joins a vaudeville troupe which includes two young men from Switzerland, one from France, and one from Italy. Alvina falls in love with the Italian, Cicio, and has sexual relations with him. Later, having left the troupe, she becomes engaged to a Lancaster physician. As the wife of this physician, Alvina would enjoy a rather enviable social position. Obedient, however, to the call of love—or sex—she returns to Cicio, marries him, and goes to settle down with him in his native village in southern Italy. Lawrence's attempt to have *The Lost Girl* serialized did not succeed. When it appeared in book form, however, he received a prize of one hundred pounds from the University of Edinburgh. Middleton Murry reviewed it, in the *Atheneum*, under the title, "The Decay of Mr. D. H. Lawrence"; and Richard Aldington calls it "the worst book Lawrence ever wrote."

In January, 1921, Lawrence and Frieda made an excursion to Sardinia. They journeyed by train to Messina and thence to Palermo, where they embarked for their destination. Their small boat rocked, but Lawrence delighted in its honest build. On the other hand he despised the crew, who seemed to have nothing to do but loaf about staring at the passengers. Their luncheon included such delicacies as oily cabbage soup and an omelette made, apparently, of leather. Scarcely better was their dinner, the main dish of which consisted of gluey polyps fried in oil. After a fitful night's rest in their tiny, airless cabin, they awoke to find themselves in view of the Sardinian shore. But Lawrence's pleasure in the spectacle was marred by the ship's carpenter, whose conversation on international politics made him feel as if someone were "stuffing wads of chewed newspaper into his ear."

Soon the Lawrences landed at Cagliari, where they found the people engaged in a carnival and where they got some decent food at last. Then, somewhat refreshed, they started north in a third-class railway carriage. They stopped overnight at a place called Mandas. From there, in the morning, they took a train that wound higher and higher into the mountains, through cork-oak trees that were stripped of their bark. In the evening they left the train at Sorgono, where they had to wait for food until an old man had finished roasting a kid over a great fire of cork-oak roots. Their room was so indescribably filthy that they were glad to leave the next morning, without tipping, on an early bus. Some of the mountain villages through which they passed were more attractive. In one of these they wit-

24

nessed a religious procession with lovely costumes. At the inn of Nuoro, home of the novelist Grazia Deledda, they had a large, clean bedroom for a change. Because the afternoon was very cold, they proceeded to warm up by getting into bed at once, whereupon the maid came in and peered at Lawrence as if he had been "a rabbit in the grass." Nuoro, like Cagliari, was holding a carnival. So much so that, on the following morning, they couldn't even get bread to eat before it was time to catch their bus. One of the passengers complained because he was obliged to pay full fare for his two little pigs, "exactly as if they had been Christians!" Pausing that noon at Siniscola, they lunched on meat that seemed to Lawrence considerably inferior to "the foot of an old worsted stocking." Towards night they arrived at Terranova, where they boarded the small steamer that was to carry them to Italy. The fore-deck was crowded with cattle and with fowls in coops. They prepared their own supper on deck with the aid of a spirit lamp. Then they sat beneath the stars for a while, wrapped up together in a Scottish shepherd's shawl. At length, as the ship had separate cabins for men and women, they had to say good-night.

Lawrence was glad, when they disembarked at Città Vecchia, to smell once more the wine-like air of Italy. He was glad also to be able to read the *Corriere della Sera* on their south-bound train. At Rome the train filled up with soldiers who had fought in vain at Fiume with D'Annunzio. Lawrence and Frieda left it in the evening at Naples, where they had a hard struggle to buy tickets for their crossing to the Sicilian port of Palermo, the starting-point of their arduous but colorful trip. Though Lawrence had hated certain things in Sardinia, he had found it more natural, more "manly" than Sicily. Now, though he hated certain

25

things in Sicily, he thought it far more civilized than Sardinia. His critical spirit was never for an instant quiet, so that he was never long contented anywhere.

On his return from Sardinia Lawrence wrote to Mrs. R. P.: "It was an exciting little trip, but one couldn't live there—one would be weary, dreary. I was very disappointed." Yet his excursion resulted in the brilliant, if ill-tempered, *Sea and Sardinia*. Lawrence wrote this book in about six weeks, and never bothered to revise it. It was Frieda, in fact, who discovered the manuscript "in the W. C." at Fontana Vecchia. Lawrence sent it in April, 1921, to Curtis Brown, through whom it was published, in the same year, by Martin Secker. *Sea and Sardinia* is one of Lawrence's best books of travel, having more unity than *Mornings in Mexico,* and being more readable than *Etruscan Places.* The interest of the narrative lies not so much in the towns and villages visited, many of which were extremely drab, as in the author's reactions to other people, whom he liked or disliked with extraordinary vigor.

In March the many-sided Lawrence learned that the Oxford University Press had published *Movements in European History,* a textbook he had written under the pseudonym of "Lawrence H. Davison."

In May Lawrence made two friends who were to stand by him for the rest of his life with the most touching loyalty. While in Capri he called at the Torre dei Quattro Venti, the villa of Earl and Achsah Brewster, American painters who had lived for many years in Europe. The Brewsters were planning to leave in the autumn for Ceylon, where Earl was to study Buddhism. Lawrence was so delighted with them and with Harwood, their small daughter, that he tried to persuade them to join him in buying a "lugger," and in going on a cruise. "He brought with him," writes

Mr. Brewster in his *Reminiscences,* "some quality of the outdoor world, from the shrubs and flowers. The sweetness of sun-dried leaves and grass seemed never to leave him." And Mrs. Brewster describes her impressions of him thus:

He moved with lithe precision, his feet alive in his shoes. . . . The nose was blunted, and from certain angles, together with his great brow, suggested the statues of Socrates. His mouth was curiously unmodelled, like those the Greeks assigned to Pan and the satyrs. . . . Again he seemed like Whistler's portrait of Carlyle.

He was, she adds, "a brave man who dared to speak his profound convictions. . . . He had a way of transmuting the dull stuff of life into cloth of gold."

In the summer of 1921, when Sicily was hot, the Lawrences went to Baden-Baden, where Frieda's mother lived. Here Lawrence wrote his *Fantasia of the Unconscious,* a psychoanalytical treatise. Of this work Hugh Kingsmill somewhat disparagingly remarks: "So far as one can salvage anything concrete out of *Fantasia of the Unconscious,* it is a belief in the possibility of re-establishing some kind of connection, once known and now forgotten, between man and the cosmos." And he adds: "This kind of speculation does not help anyone to live, any more than pondering the law of gravity helps a man to climb a mountain."

July and August the Lawrences spent with Frieda's younger sister Johanna, her husband, and her children, at their villa in Zell-am-See on a mountain lake in Austria. It was about this time that Lawrence was completing *Aaron's Rod,* a short novel highly praised by Middleton Murry, but considered by most critics to be structurally defective. Aaron, the chief character, is secretary of an English miners' union. Because his wife seems physically unresponsive he leaves his home and tries to live by playing the flute in London. There he meets a writer named Lilley, with whom,

27

after the War is ended, he goes to Italy. His affair with a *marquesa,* in Florence, leaves the unfortunate fellow as dissatisfied as he was in the beginning. The novel is to a large extent autobiographical, and the first part contains some excellent satire.

Though Frieda was having a wonderful time at Zell-am-See, Lawrence, perhaps disturbed by the presence of the handsome young officers who surrounded her, induced her to go with him to Florence, where it was still, of course, quite hot. They stayed for three weeks in their friend Nelly Morrison's flat, which was located in a house supposed to have been that of Romola. While they were in Florence Don and Catherine Carswell, who had arrived from England, came to visit them for a week. "Though I never felt more drawn to Lawrence," writes Catherine Carswell, in *The Savage Pilgrimage* "there was about him something restless, remote and even impatient, which blurred the approach and made me doubt sadly once or twice if my own sympathy found any response." This is interesting, for wherever Lawrence went he was always writing Catherine that he wanted her to join him, "in a little while," and of course with her husband Don and her little boy John Patrick. Catherine introduced Lawrence to some Anglo-Italian cousins whom she had in Florence, but he didn't like them, and they had never heard of him, seemingly being ignorant of modern English writers with the exception of Oscar Wilde, Hall Caine, Marie Corelli, and possibly John Galsworthy. On Lawrence's thirty-seventh birthday he and Frieda entertained the Carswells at supper in their flat. During the meal Lawrence praised the *Corriere della Sera* at the expense of the *London Times,* and deplored the immoral behavior of the young Italians on the opposite bank of the Arno.

During this summer of 1921 the Fascist order was on the

march, and fighting was a common occurrence in the streets of Florence. Whenever a shot rang out, Lawrence declared, the people "ran up the fronts of the houses like flies, and down into the earth like mice." When Don and Catherine Carswell left, it was agreed that the Lawrences would meet them a little later in Siena. But Lawrence, after a hasty glance at Siena, "hated it so much that he could not bear to stay another day."

In September Lawrence and Frieda came together to visit the Brewsters at their Capri villa. A good time seems to have been had by everyone. Lawrence helped Harwood with her herbarium, imitated an aesthetic lady playing upon the psaltery, and made fun—though not unkindly—of Achsah's painting of St. Francis preaching to the birds. When the Lawrences returned to Taormina, Earl accompanied them as far as Naples. Shortly after his arrival at Fontana Vecchia, in October, Lawrence wrote to Edward Garnett:

I still feel battered after all the summer travels. . . . The north always makes me feel weak and hopeless. . . . I'm so thankful to be back in the South, beyond the Straits of Messina, in the shadow of Etna, and with the Ionian Sea in front: the lovely, lovely dawn-sea where the sun does nothing but rise toward Greece.

Back in Taormina, Lawrence became interested in translating some of the novels and tales of Giovanni Verga, including *Cavalleria Rusticana*. He wrote to Catherine Carswell and to Edward Garnett asking them to find out whether Verga's novels (*I Malavoglia* and *Maestro don Gesualdo*) and stories (*Novelle Rusticane*) had already been done into English. *Don Gesualdo* had been, as he discovered, but so long ago that he resolved to make a fresh translation. Presently he wrote to Curtis Brown, his literary agent: "I am nearly half-way through the translation of a Sicilian novel, *Maestro don Gesualdo,* by Giovanni Verga. He just died—aged 82—in Catania. I think he is so very good." Concerning Lawrence's translations, Catherine Carswell has this to say:

Lawrence has never had full credit as a translator. He had a gift similar to that of the late C. K. Scott-Moncrieff. He could enter into the meaning of a highly individual outlook on life that was other than his own and expressed in a difficult idiom. Had he not been novelist and poet in his own right, he might have earned good money, and easy fame and high ungrudging acknowledgment as a translator. He is of the first rank.

Lawrence's life in Taormina was not, of course, entirely pleasant. He learned that his novel *Women in Love* had been described in *John Bull* as "a shameless study of sex depravity which in direct proportion to the skill of its literary execution becomes unmentionably vile." Simultaneously he was threatened with a suit for libel by Philip Heseltine, who charged that Lawrence's effeminate character Halliday was a representation of himself. Heseltine accepted the publisher's settlement of fifty pounds, and consoled himself, it seems, by growing a beard.

In November Mabel Dodge Luhan, of Taos, New Mexico, wrote to tell Lawrence how much she had enjoyed *Sea and Sardinia.* She urged him to come to Taos, where he and Frieda would be her guests, and study the Pueblo Indians there. With Mrs. Luhan's letter went an Indian necklace which was offered as a gift to Frieda, and which was supposed to have some magic property that would draw the Lawrences to Taos. Frieda accepted the invitation eagerly. But Lawrence, in his own reply, made all sorts of cautious inquiries about the cost of living, about the possible presence of "sub-arty" people, and about the nature of the Indians. He wrote to Donald Carswell:

A woman called Mabel Dodge Sterne Luhan writes from Taos, New Mexico, saying we can have a furnished adobe house there . . . if we'll only go. It seems Taos is on a mountain—7,000 feet up—and 23 miles from a railway, and has a tribe of 600 free Indians who she says are . . . sun-worshippers, rain-makers, and unspoiled. It sounds rather fun.

But a little later, in a letter to Catherine Carswell, Lawrence said:

I have once more gone back on my plan. I shrink as yet from the States. . . . I want to go east before I go west; go west *via* the east. I have a friend called Brewster, who went with wife and child from here last autumn to Kandy, Ceylon. He has got a big old ramshackle bungalow there, and is studying Pali and Buddhism at the Buddhist monastery, and asks me to come. So I shall go there.

Then there began a seemingly interminable correspondence between Mable Dodge Luhan and Lawrence—the former gently but firmly urging, the latter eternally withdrawing, evading, procrastinating. Lawrence's letters express an indecision that results, in spite of his courageous attitude toward many things, from fear. He is afraid of passing through the blatant, blaring metropolis of New York, and wonders if he cannot enter the United States by way of New Orleans instead. He is afraid of treading on American soil without an escort, and wishes that Mrs. Luhan might meet him and his wife in India. In the meantime the two correspondents indulged in an exchange of books and in a discussion of psychiatric subjects. Both the fascination and the terror that America inspired in Lawrence are powerfully expressed in these lines from his poem, "The Evening Land":

31

> You have cajoled the souls of millions of us,
> America
> Why won't you cajole my soul?
> I wish you would.
> I confess I am afraid of you.

In February, 1922, Lawrence and Frieda abandoned Fontana Vecchia, the villa they had occupied for two years in Taormina, and went by way of Palermo to Naples, where they embarked for Ceylon. Just as Lawrence would have regretted it if he had decided to go to America or to remain in Sicily, so he regretted his decision to go to India. But once aboard the *S. S. Osterley* and out of sight of land, his spirits rose. The luxury of the vessel, and the efficiency with which it was manned, delighted him. He rejoiced in the fact that it was a British ship, and that he himself was a Briton. The natural result of his satisfaction was that he was at his very best with the other passengers. He was quite charming; he even danced!

The Lawrences disembarked at the port of Colombo, in Ceylon. There they were met by Earl Brewster, who traveled with them to Kandy and welcomed them to "Ardnaree," the bungalow in which he was living with his wife and daughter. It was a spacious house, nestling in a grove of palm trees on a hill above the town. Frieda exclaimed at once that it was the loveliest spot in the world, and Lawrence declared: "I shall never leave it!" One of his first acts was to toss his watch, which had ceased running, into the middle of the lake. Thereafter, although he had no watch, he wore one-half of Earl Brewster's watch-chain, which was, he said, too long for Earl. The two men wandered together through the forest, which teemed with animals, snakes, and birds. They were quite congenial, but Lawrence did not sympathize with Brewster's Buddhistic propensities.

"Oh," he exclaimed whenever he saw the statue of the seated Buddha, "how I wish he would stand up!" Of course he refused to join the Brewsters when they removed their hats and shoes to make offerings in Buddhist shrines.

While he and Frieda were living with their friends in Ceylon, Lawrence was completing his translation of the short stories of Giovanni Verga. As usual, he did his writing in a school-boy's copy-book, undisturbed by the conversation and laughter of the others. When he had finished the manuscript he sent it off to his publisher without making a single correction. Lawrence brought home many a treasure from the bazaar, but he would never allow a rickshaw boy to pull him up the hill in the heat. It rained every day at exactly 10 A.M. and 4 P.M. Everyone was depressed by the dampness and the mould. "The east is not for me," Lawrence wrote to Lady Cynthia Asquith, "the curious sensitiveness of the native people, their black, bottomless, hopeless eyes—and the heads of elephants and buffaloes poking out of primeval mud . . . makes me feel rather sick." At the end of April the Lawrences and the Brewsters left Ceylon, the former traveling east, the latter west. It would be four years before they saw one another again.

Australia was the Lawrences' next stopping place. Landing at Fremantle, they went on to Perth. Here Lawrence met the Mrs. Skinner with whom he was to collaborate on *The Boy in the Bush*. The strange "primeval" quality of the land impressed him. The sky seemed very blue, and the air extraordinarily pure. Lawrence and Frieda crossed the continent to Sydney. But the city had a certain crudeness that made Lawrence violently homesick for Europe. Europe, that he had been so anxious, a short time previously, to leave! For the rest of the summer, however, they had a bungalow in Thirroul, a village forty miles south of Sydney

33

on the Pacific. Although the bungalow was dirty when they took it, they scrubbed the floors until they gleamed. After such labors it was heavenly to have a swim, or just to lie on the broad verandah watching the mountainous waves come rolling in. While he was in Australia Lawrence wrote his novel *Kangaroo,* in which the characters Richard Lovatt Somers and Harriet represent himself and Frieda. In this novel Lawrence tells about the poverty and persecution they had suffered in Cornwall, during the First World War. He touchingly reveals, moreover, his awareness of his own shortcomings and of the sorrows he had brought his wife.

Perhaps Lawrence tired of Australia, as he seemed to tire eventually of every haven which he visited. Perhaps the will of Mabel Dodge Luhan, symbolized by the necklace she had sent to Frieda, was drawing him towards New Mexico. At any event, the Lawrences sailed in August for San Francisco, whence they would travel by rail to the mysterious Indian citadel of Taos.

LAWRENCE AND FRIEDA arrived in Taos, New Mexico, in
September, 1922. They had come from Australia by way of
San Francisco, and had left the train at Lamy, sixteen miles
from Santa Fe. At Lamy they were met by their hostess,
Mabel Dodge Luhan. During the whole of the previous year
Mrs. Luhan had been urging Lawrence to come to Taos, so
that he might become acquainted with the Pueblo Indians
and interpret them to the English-speaking world. And Lawrence had reached New Mexico at last, but only after a
journey round the globe.

When the Lawrences descended from their train at Lamy,
Mrs. Luhan and Tony, her Indian husband, saw a tall, thin
man with a red beard, and a stoutish woman who looked
and dressed like a German *hausfrau*. The meal that they
ate in the Fred Harvey restaurant passed in embarrassed
silence, while the two women measured each other as
women will. To Mabel the air seemed charged with elec-
tricity, for in *Lorenzo in Taos* she writes: "We got seated
in a row at the counter, the atmosphere splitting and crack-
ling all about us from the singular crash of our meeting.
There was a vibratory disturbance around our neighbor-
hood like an upheaval in nature."

At last they all got into Tony's car and were driven

across the desert, blooming with gray-green sagebrush, towards Santa Fe. Lawrence sat up front with Tony, while Frieda and Mabel occupied the rear seat together. From where the women sat, Tony's broad back loomed up like the rock of Gibraltar. "What a strong man Tony is!" cried Frieda. "How wonderful it must be to have a man like that to lean on!" At this remark poor Lawrence, who couldn't help overhearing it, stiffened ominously. They had not driven very far when something went wrong with the engine and the car stopped. Tony, getting out and raising the hood, began to tinker. After he had labored for some time with no result, Frieda turned to Lawrence and said: "You're not doing a thing! Why don't you get out and help him?" Lawrence, who knew nothing about machinery and cared even less, gave her a glance that was charged with the wrath of hell. Just then the engine started with a roar. When they asked Tony what had been the matter with it, he said he thought that there must have been a snake inside!

In Santa Fe, because all the hotels were full, Mabel prevailed upon the poet Witter Bynner to put the Lawrences up for the night while she and Tony accepted the hospitality of some other friends. Later on Lawrence was to maintain very cordial relations with Bynner, and with Bynner's friend Willard Johnson, another writer, who was known as "Spud." That night, however, he grumbled because he was forced to stay with strangers; the following day he made disparaging remarks about "the type of man who cannot face the problems of the world, and who hides himself in some snug corner, such as Santa Fe, to get away from them."

In the morning, after a breakfast prepared by Lawrence and Frieda, they drove for sixty miles through the canyon of the Rio Grande, until finally they emerged, seven thousand feet up, in the splendor of Taos Valley. Their first glimpse of the valley is described as follows by Frieda Lawrence: "Coming out of the canyon to the *mesa* is an unforgettable experience, with all the deep mountains sitting mysteriously around in a ring, and so much sky." But the sky was dark, and suddenly a blinding flash of lightning shot from a black cloud to a mountain peak. For a moment there was silence, while the whole world seemed to wait. Then came a crash of thunder so terrific that the occupants of the car crouched down with their hands pressed tight against their ears. Years later Frieda and Mabel and Tony would remember this sign, this omen, that marked the arrival of D. H. Lawrence in Taos Valley.

Mabel had a brown adobe ranch house on a hillside overlooking Taos village. She quartered the Lawrences in a guest house, also of adobe and colorfully furnished with Indian pottery and rugs. Lawrence and Frieda liked Taos immediately. It was already the seat of an important colony of American artists. A few miles north stood the two five-story houses of the Taos Indians, and a few miles south was the Mexican, or Spanish-American, village of Ranchos de Taos, with its Penitente church and its *moradas*—Penitente chapels—tucked away in the folds of the hills.

Shortly after Lawrence's arrival in Taos, Tony took him and Bessie Wilkinson, a friend of Mabel's from Buffalo, to see an Indian dance. His absence gave Mabel a chance to get acquainted with Frieda. Mabel asked many questions about Lawrence, and Frieda answered them with her customary frankness. "It seems to me," Mabel remarked, "that Lawrence receives all of his impressions of life through you. You are his eyes and his ears, without which it would be impossible for him to know the world."

"That is true," said Frieda, "It is only through me that Lawrence can get his impressions of the world outside.

People say that he is a genius, and he is. But how could he write, except for me?" Lawrence, immediately on his return, sensed that he had been discussed, and became quite angry about it.

Concerning his trip Lawrence wrote, in a letter to Martin Secker, his London publisher: "We got here last week and since then I have been away motoring for five days into the Apache country to see an Apache dance. It is a weird country, and I feel a great stranger still." And in the post-script of a letter to E. M. Forster: "These are Red Indians— so different from the grain-growing Indians of Taos—yet Chinesey. I haven't got the hang of them yet." He described his impressions of the Indian dance in "Indians and an Englishman," an article published in the *Dial* for February, 1923, and in the *Adelphi* for November of the same year. The article reveals his awareness of the immense gulf that separates the "civilized" white man from the brown "savage."

From the Indian dance Lawrence returned to Taos and a life that Mabel filled with exciting new experiences. There were visits to the Pueblo, and baths in a pool of water "charged with radium." Lawrence learned to ride an Indian pony. Although he was unafraid and always kept his seat, he rode bent forward in a painful manner that made Tony laugh. In the interims between their excursions Frieda busied herself with domestic tasks, like boiling some wild plums contributed to them by the Indians. The air was ever fragrant with the smell of the *piñón* wood that the natives burned both for cooking and for heating. Sometimes, in the evening, a group of Indians would come to Mabel's studio and beat their drums and tread their strange, wild dance, in which, presently the white people too would join. It was hot—with a dry heat—in the daytime, but delightfully cool at night. Though Lawrence relished all of this, there were moments when he yearned for Australia—the very place he had been so anxious, a few weeks previously, to get away from!

The Pueblo Indians had, of course, been converted by the Spaniards to Catholicism. In Taos Pueblo there was a chapel which contained a statue of the Holy Virgin. On September thirtieth, the festival of San Gerónimo, who was the Indians' patron saint, the statue was carried through the streets of Taos in the midst of much rejoicing and even revelry. This blend of pagan and Christian elements interested Lawrence intensely. He was interested also in the ensuing Indian dance. For this the men were clad in foxskins, and the women followed them with rattles made of gourds containing seeds. In the course of the dance the Indians blew eagle feathers upwards toward the sun, as if to impart to it power which they hoped would be returned to them.

Mabel thought that Lawrence had very little "sense of leisure." In the morning, after finishing his housework, he would slip outside and go to some secluded spot to write. It was ordinarily he who prepared the noonday meal and who cleaned up after it. Then, unless some excursion was planned for the afternoon, he would busy himself with carpentry or with other odd jobs, which he seemed to consider no less important than his writing. In the evening he would frequently organize charades, at which he was very clever and which he enjoyed tremendously. And yet, while Lawrence was savoring all of this, his critical faculty was, as usual, working overtime. For in the postscript of a letter to Catherine Carswell he says:

In my opinion a "gentle" life with John Patrick and Don, and a gentle faith in life itself, is far better than these women in breeches and riding-boots and sombreros, and money and motorcars and wild west. It is all inwardly a hard stone and nothingness.

Lawrence strove to woo Mabel away from "money and motorcars and wild west," and to mold her into something closer to his heart's desire. He induced her to discard her flowing gowns in favor of peasant bodices and dirndls. In order to please him she affected pink-and-white checked gingham aprons. On her hands and knees she scrubbed her living room floor—or half of it—with a bucket of hot water and a cake of crude brown soap. She tried her hand at baking bread. It turned out badly, but Lawrence was magnanimous about it.

Mabel, knowing that Lawrence hated publicity, and that he particularly objected to "arty" people, endeavored to prevent any encroachment upon his privacy. But Lawrence, with exasperating perversity, complained that he was being neglected, and invited several members of the Taos colony to call. Sooner or later one of the men, who had somehow got the idea that Lawrence relished "sex," was sure to tell a smutty joke, complete with a liberal sprinkling of the usual four-letter words. Lawrence, at this, would become enraged. But when Mabel asked him why he insisted on inviting these individuals to his house, he invariably replied: "One must *know* people. One can't shut oneself off from the world."

Very shortly after Lawrence's arrival in Taos, he and Mabel Dodge Luhan had conceived the plan of a novel to be written by him and to be based on her achievement of peace and self-fulfilment among the Indians of Taos Valley. The novel was to begin at the time when Mabel had left New York to come to New Mexico, and was to describe her relations with the artist Maurice Sterne as well as her ultimate decision to join her life to that of Tony Luhan. Lawrence asked Mabel to supply him with information on many points, not omitting even those things that she might prefer to have forgotten. The novel was to include a certain number of Mabel's poems, and perhaps an autobiographical fragment that she herself had composed already. The two collaborators held their conferences on the flat roof of Mabel's house, from which they could look across the yellow desert to the blue mountains of the Sangre de Cristo Range. Before long Lawrence expressed his apprehension concerning the way in which Frieda might feel about his intimacy with Mabel. And indeed, when he returned to his adobe house one day, Frieda stood in the doorway to greet him "with arms akimbo." She insisted that Lawrence and Mabel, if they wished to work together, must do it in the Lawrences' house. As this seemed unreasonable to Mabel, the collaboration ceased, Lawrence never wrote the novel, and Mabel never realized her desire to be painted by him against the background of Taos Valley. New Mexico inspired Lawrence to write only a number of poems and essays, his tale "The Princess," and the concluding episode of his novelette *St. Mawr*. It was not until later, when he was in Old Mexico, that he used Mabel—or an adaptation of Mabel—as the heroine of his novel *The Plumed Serpent* and of his story *The Woman Who Rode Away*.

Now Mabel began to write long letters to Lawrence, until she learned that Lawrence, "just to make everything square and open," was showing her letters to his wife. Then the correspondence, like the collaboration, ceased. Even when Lawrence and Frieda went together to evening parties at Mabel's house, some sort of tension was sure to develop. Occasionally Frieda, fancying herself ignored, would sit and gaze contemptuously at her husband through half-closed eyes, a cigarette drooping from the corner of

41

her mouth. Lawrence would order her to throw the cigarette away; Frieda would flare up at him with some angry retort; Lawrence would make an insulting comment on her appearance; and finally Frieda would rise and leave the party, with Lawrence following at her heels. Mabel writes of Lawrence as "a frail cargo that he hauls through life with perpetual distaste." She deplores his "desperate and hopeless bondage to one who was the antithesis of himself and his predilections." "Like a lively lamb tied to a solid stake," she declares, "he frisked and pulled in agony, not Promethean so much as Panic."

One day Mabel criticized Frieda for her possessive attitude toward Lawrence. Frieda replied: "Try it then yourself, living with a genius, see what it is like and how easy it is, take him if you can." Shortly after this Lawrence heard, rightly or wrongly, that Mabel had accused him of "sponging" on her. This made him so furious that he vowed to pay the rent on the little adobe house and to leave at once. The Lawrences did leave Taos, about three months after their arrival, but they went to live at a ranch that Mabel owned, Del Monte, seventeen miles away and at an altitude of nearly nine thousand feet.

Shortly before their departure for Del Monte Ranch, the Lawrences had met two Danish artists, Merrild and Götzsche, who had been introduced to them by Walter Ufer, one of the leading local painters and head of the Taos Art Association. Merrild and Götzsche, ill at ease in the commercial atmosphere of New York, had set out for California in a second-hand Model T Ford. Their trip came to an end, temporarily at least, in New Mexico; for it was soon agreed that they would drive Lawrence and Frieda up to Del Monte, and that they would be loaned a separate cabin there in which they too could spend the winter.

The Del Monte Ranch consisted of some 1,500 acres of timberland, and grazed over a hundred head of cattle. It was managed for Mrs. Luhan by a young couple named Hawk, whom Lawrence liked. Soon after his arrival there in November, 1922, he wrote Catherine Carswell a letter in which his impressions—some of them conflicting—are recorded in a very interesting way:

We have an old 5-room log cabin on this big wild ranch on the Rocky foothills—the snow mountains behind, a vast landscape below . . . desert, and then more mountains west, far off in Arizona. . . . The coyotes come down howling at evening. . . . We all chop down trees for our burning, and go off riding together. Altogether it is ideal. But *innerlich,* there is nothing. . . . All this outside life—and marvellous country—and it all means so little to one. I don't quite know what it is one wants because the ordinary society and "talk" in Europe are weary enough. . . . I know now I don't want to live anywhere very long. . . . I seem to have a fair sale over here—*Women in Love* going into 15,000. Why do they read me? But, anyhow, they *do* read me, which is more than England does.

In the lines above poor Lawrence reveals his dissatisfaction both with Europe and with America, and his realization that he could never hope to be completely happy either in the Old World or in the New. Yet for the rest of his life, as Anthony West remarks, he was to continue his quest for *Rananim*—"a community of those who had given up the world to go into a place apart, to live life as Lawrence believed it should be lived."

The satisfaction of "the Danes," as Götzsche and Merrild were called, on moving up to Del Monte Ranch was quite untarnished by any metaphysical qualms. As Merrild, in *A Poet and Two Painters,* writes, they thoroughly enjoyed the carpenter work that had to be done, both on the Lawrances' cabin and on their own:

43

We worked hard at roofing, carpentering, plastering, glazing, paperhanging (*sic*), painting, whitewashing, etc. Frieda was busy sewing curtains and the like. Lawrence enjoyed himself thoroughly doing all these odd jobs. It felt good to be a labourer. One of us suggested that we form a Del Monte Local of the I.W.W.

Because the winter would undoubtedly be severe, it was necessary to lay in a plentiful supply of firewood. In the forest Lawrence and the Danes discovered a huge dead tree and felled it. The process of sawing it up, with a two-handed saw, kept them busy for many days. And many more days were needed, after the logs had been hauled to the ranch, to chop them into a handy size.

The ranch, especially when the trail lay deep in snow, was rather inaccessible, so that their food had to be of the simplest sort. They had porridge for breakfast, salted meat, potatoes, and apple sauce for dinner, and maybe porridge again for supper. But now and then Lawrence would cook delicious English dishes, as well as bake the bread. He always insisted on brewing tea himself. Washing the clothes was Frieda's special province. She loved to scrub great piles of linen until it actually looked whiter than the snow on which it was laid to dry.

After their creek had frozen, the problem of the water supply became acute. They had to use melted snow for drinking and for cooking, and they bathed in the snow itself. Every two weeks or so they would drive or ride to the hot springs, twenty miles away, for a real bath. There they would soak themselves in the warm, supposedly radioactive water, emerge to scrub their bodies with lathery soap, and then plunge back into the pool for a luxurious rinse. Once home, the men would cut each other's hair, an operation in which Lawrence took the greatest pride, and which he performed in one of Frieda's aprons, with a pair of spectacles on the end of his nose.

Every day, after the chores were done, the Danes devoted themselves to sketching and painting. Lawrence composed the remaining poems that were to appear in *Birds, Beasts and Flowers,* and answered the many letters he received from friends in various parts of the world. Once he played chess with Merrild, but was so badly beaten that he never consented to play again. Götzsche owned a violin, and Merrild had discovered, in some corner, an ancient flute. One evening the four friends gave a concert, Lawrence using a piece of paper and a comb, Frieda a pair of pot-covers from the kitchen. The three men often engaged in lengthy philosophical discussions. With regard to these talks Merrild has written: "I confess to myself that it is those hours I treasure as among the most precious memories of my life." Lawrence expressed the same ideas, on these occasions, that he expressed in his letters and in his books. One of his favorite subjects was art. In this connection he told the Danes how he had learned to draw by copying, ever since his boyhood, the paintings of the masters, especially those of the Italian school. The Danes found most of Lawrence's beliefs alarmingly corrosive. However Merrild agreed with him when he said:

I believe:
That I am I.
That my soul is a dark forest.
That my known self will never be more than a little clearing in the forest.
That gods, strange gods, come forth from the forest into the clearing of my known self, and then go back.
That I must have the courage to let them come and go.

45

That I will never let mankind put anything over on me, but that I will try always to recognize and submit to the gods in me and the gods in other men and women.

There is my creed. He who runs may read. He who prefers to crawl, or go by gasoline, can call it rot.

Though Hawk, the manager of the ranch, subscribed to a daily newspaper, Lawrence never read it. That he was preoccupied less by social problems than by individual ones is shown in these remarks to Merrild:

The great social change interests me and troubles me, but it is not my field. I know a change is coming—and I know we must have a more generous, more human system, based on the life value and not on the money values. That I know. My field is to know the feelings inside a man, and to make new feelings conscious.

In a letter to Gilbert Seldes, Lawrence expresses himself further with regard to the future of western civilization:

I feel about U.S.A. as I vaguely felt a long time ago; that there is a vast, unreal, intermediary thing intervening between the real thing which was Europe and the next real thing, which will probably be in America, but which isn't yet, at all. Seems to me a vast death-happening must come first. But probably it is here in America (I don't say just U.S.A.) that the quick will keep alive and come through.

Lawrence was expecting a visit from his publisher, Thomas Seltzer. Accordingly he asked Götzsche to do a portrait of him, and Merrild to help him with designs and illustrations for *Kangaroo, The Captain's Doll, Studies in Classic American Literature,* and *Birds, Beasts and Flowers.* When Seltzer and his wife arrived, the Danes regaled them with cabbage soup, fried rabbit, and apple sauce with milk. Lawrence sang Christmas carols. Even so, Seltzer, forced to keep an eye on publishing costs, declined a number of the illustrations. But later, in a letter to Merrild, he paid

Lawrence one of the finest tributes that he ever received:

Lawrence was as great a man as he was a writer. In every aspect of life he was natural, without pose, and, at bottom, sane. Follow him in the kitchen when he cooks, when he washes and irons his own underwear, when he does chores for Frieda. Observe him when he walks with you in the country, when he is in the company of people whom he likes . . . how natural he is in every movement and yet how distinguished . . . because he is natural. . . . So many people dwell only on his fierce outbreaks. But to me his outbreaks . . . were not of the essence of him. The times and his environment are more to blame than himself.

On Christmas Eve, at the Taos Pueblo, there was an Indian dance. Lawrence wrote to Mabel Dodge Luhan asking if he and the Seltzers and the Danes might stay at her house for a night or two. She answered that, since she was entertaining only members of her own family, this would be impossible. The Danes attempted to persuade Lawrence to go with them to Taos anyway, and stay with somebody else, but he refused. Nevertheless, when they reached the pueblo at sundown, there he was. He hadn't been able to resist the dancing among the bonfires, the chanting, and the drums.

During the winter that the Lawrences spent at Del Monte there were many storms, but in between them the air was clear and dry and the skies were blue. One day the three men tried to climb to the peak of Lobo Mountain. They had to turn back because Lawrence, though he did his very best, simply did not possess the necessary physical stamina. Now and then he had to stay in bed for a day with a cold. On these occasions he would drink sage tea, and when Merrild had a cold he tried to make him drink some, too. In the bitter weather it was often very hard to start the car. They had to prime the cylinders with gasoline, and pour hot water into the radiator.

In the middle of the winter, when the roads were extremely precarious, Lawrence had to attend to some business over the state line in Colorado. Frieda and the Danes accompanied him in "Lizzie," their Model T Ford. On the way back, as they were following a narrow road around a mountain, they encountered a Mexican coming in the opposite direction with a wagon. The Mexican gave them very little room, and as they tried to pass him two of their wheels slipped off the road, so that the axles of their car rested on the edge of a precipice hundreds of feet high. The Mexican continued calmly on his way. After creeping gingerly from the car, they managed somehow to hoist it back again to the road, thankful for their narrow escape from death.

Lawrence's Spanish, which he had been digging out of an antiquated grammar, wasn't as good as his German or his Italian. Nevertheless he kept trying it on the Mexicans, saying the words over and over until they understood. He even tried to teach Spanish to Götzsche and Merrild. But Frieda poked fun at what she called his old-fashioned methods of pedagogy, especially when he used such sentences as: "My Aunt Mary has a bird."

Already Lawrence, weary of giving Spanish lessons, was planning to go with Frieda in the spring to Mexico, where he hoped to find a place for himself and his friends to live. After he had found it he would send for Merrild and Götzsche, and they would come and help him grow bananas. "When we have ourselves firmly established," he explained, "then we can add one or two more of our friends at a time and let the thing grow slowly into full being, and the new life will grow and spread until it embraces the whole world." Meanwhile he was learning about the country from Terry's *Guide*.

Lawrence had forbidden Frieda to send letters to her

children. Whenever friends wrote to her about them, he would rant and rave. He objected also to her smoking—or at least to her *way* of smoking—with a cigarette drooping from the corner of her mouth. One day he seized her package of cigarettes and flung it into the fire. Frieda, fearing that he might confiscate her entire supply, gave the Danes a carton of cigarettes to keep for her. Presently Lawrence attempted to atone for his behavior by baking cakes.

Pips, a French bull-terrier owned by Lawrence, suddenly deserted him and went to live with the Danes. He was very unhappy about this until, just as suddenly, she came back again to his cabin. When Pips got in heat, however, she left her master once more, to wander into the forest with the Danes' airedale. Then, if we may credit the story told by Merrild, something happened that revealed the sickness in Lawrence's mind. Waiting until Pips, in a joyous and playful mood, returned to him, he pounced upon her, struck her, kicked her, and might have even killed her, had not Merrild intervened. And yet, as Merrild says, the normal Lawrence was always kind to animals. He even cursed the Danes for shooting rabbits. Lawrence himself, apparently unaware of the strangeness of his relationship with the dog, describes it graphically in the poem "Bibbles," from *Birds, Beasts and Flowers.*

It was at about this time that Lawrence learned, through Middleton Murry, of Katherine Mansfield's death in Gourdjieff's theosophical retreat at Fontainebleau. He answered:

I got your note just now . . . about Katherine. Yes, it is something gone out of our lives. . . . I . . . asked Seltzer to send you *Fantasia of the Unconscious.* I wanted Katherine to read it. She'll know, though. The dead don't die. They look on and help. . . . I wish it needn't all have been as it has been; I do wish it.

49

On the tenth of February, 1923, the thermometer went down to twenty-five degrees below zero. Because of the intense cold, and because Lawrence didn't encourage visitors, few people came to call at Del Monte Ranch. One afternoon Witter Bynner, the poet, who had driven up to Taos from Santa Fe, dropped in. On another afternoon it was Mabel Dodge Luhan who came. When they heard her car approaching, Lawrence and the Danes took to the woods, like naughty boys, leaving Frieda to face the music by herself. In spite of Lawrence's behavior, Mabel invited him and Frieda and the Danes to see another Indian dance, at the pueblo of San Ildefonso. But Lawrence, feeling that she didn't really want the Danes, declined. Frieda was thankful, and the Danes were filled with glee.

In March Lawrence decided that it was time to go to Mexico. He gave the Danes a number of things he wouldn't be needing any more. When he closed his cabin they closed theirs too, for they felt that life at the ranch could never be the same without him. They all drove down together to Taos. There the Danes would remain, preparing an exhibition of their paintings, until warmer weather permitted them to resume their trek to California. The Lawrences, after saying goodbye to their friends, left Taos for Santa Fe, which was to be the starting point of their Mexican journey.

CHAPALA

LAWRENCE visited Mexico twice, first in 1923, and again in 1924. At the time of his first visit he and Frieda had been living for six months, as we have seen, in the mountains of New Mexico. After a winter spent at an altitude of nearly nine thousand feet, they were eager to taste the blessings of a gentler climate. Of their train trip Frieda writes:

The journey across the lonely desert had been strange. The stations were only a few miserable houses and a big water tank, and fine dust blew in at the window of the car, filling one's eyes and ears and nose, all one's pores, with very fine sand.

On arriving in Mexico City, in March, the Lawrences went to stay at a first-class American hotel. Frieda was delighted, after all the privations she had suffered at the ranch, to have at last a taste of luxury. But Lawrence decided that the other guests were for the most part people of questionable manners and of even more dubious morality. At his insistence, therefore, they moved to the less expensive, but possibly more virtuous, Hotel Monte Carlo. There they were joined by two friends whom they had met in Santa Fe, the poet Witter Bynner and Bynner's friend "Spud" Johnson, editor of an esoteric magazine, *The Laughing Horse*. Bynner calls the Monte Carlo a bohemian

51

Italian hostelry, "where a headquartering vaudeville troupe aired its trained apes and dogs and cockatoos under the washlines on the roof," but where one could enjoy "perfect minestrone, ravioli, spaghetti, and Chianti wine from straw-wrapped bottles." During his stay in Mexico City Lawrence spent many evenings writing miscellaneous essays to be posted, in the morning, to his agent. Often Frieda and his friends would be chatting away in the same room. "We marvelled constantly," Bynner says, "at his ability to be writing and talking at the same moment."

Lawrence thought the city rather tawdry. In a letter to Catherine Carswell he called it "ramshackle and Americanized." The parties to which he was invited by American and English residents bored him. The frescoes of the modern Mexican artists seemed to him ugly, shot through and through with political propaganda, and utterly devoid of a sense of humor. When Señor Vasconcelos, the Minister of Education, kept him waiting for some time and then asked a postponement of their interview, he stalked out of the Minister's office and could not be persuaded to return. It was in this unfortunate state of mind that he was taken, on Easter Sunday, to see a bullfight.

Lawrence would describe his impressions of the bullfight later, in the opening pages of *The Plumed Serpent*. He was, needless to say, completely disgusted with it. The *toreros* themselves, with their smooth-shaven faces and their pigtails, reminded him of fat-hipped women. The proletarian spectators, who amused themselves by tossing banana skins in his direction, infuriated him. The killing of the bulls seemed to him cowardly and sadistic; and when an old, blindfolded horse was gored he rose, in the midst of jibes and jeers from the Mexicans, and stormed out of the bull ring.

The archeological treasures in the National Museum were another matter. Lawrence became intensely interested in the great stone carvings salvaged from the pre-Columbian past. He and Frieda enjoyed their excursions to various shrines of Aztec civilization, notably to the Pyramid of the Sun at Teotihuacan. Lawrence sent Catherine Carswell a postcard photograph of himself, Frieda, and Bynner standing on top of the pyramid. On the postcard Lawrence had written that Teotihuacan was even more impressive than Pompeii or the Roman Forum. Frieda was suddenly terrified when, near the pyramid, she stumbled accidentally on a great stone snake, green with turquoise eyes.

At the end of April, after a brief excursion with Frieda and the others to Puebla, Orizaba, and Tehuacan, Lawrence went to Guadalajara, and from there to Chapala, on the lake of the same name. The Lake of Chapala is fifty miles long, and completely surrounded by imposing mountains. Along its beautiful and solitary shores there are only a few small fishing villages. The town of Chapala, however, is a popular vacation resort for Mexicans from Guadalajara. It has an attractive market square, three inns, and a number of villas which overlook the Lake. This was to be the scene of Lawrence's novel, *The Plumed Serpent*. In Chapala, where he was joined by his wife and friends, Lawrence rented a house belonging to the Hotel Palmera (*not* "Palinera," as it is called by several of Lawrence's biographers), at Zaragoza No. 4. The Hotel Palmera is now the Hotel Nido, and no longer owns the house where Lawrence lived. Moreover, the house itself is extremely difficult to identify, since all the numbers on the Calle Zaragoza have been changed. The Lawrences enjoyed their flower-filled veranda where Lawrence lounged barefooted and in shirt-sleeves. To do their cooking they had engaged an intelligent

53

and pleasant Mexican girl named Isabel. Out of sight but close at hand were nearly all of Isabel's male and female relatives: Carmen, María, Daniel, Pedro, and Francisco.

Lawrence's letters to his friends, while he was living in Chapala and writing *The Plumed Serpent,* indicate very clearly his preoccupations and his state of mind. In a letter to Curtis Brown, his London literary agent, he writes that he has begun a new novel and that he hopes to finish the first draft early in July. He writes to Middleton Murry that he has found Lake Chapala a better place in which to work than Mexico City. Murry had started a new shilling monthly, *Adelphi,* and had asked Lawrence to contribute to it. Lawrence replied that within two days he would send him the opening pages of his novel, which described a bull-fight. He added that someone in Chapala had offered to be his partner in establishing a banana plantation, but that he hesitated to embark on such a venture, especially without seeing England again first. Here we have a touch of Lawrence's characteristic longing to escape from England, his longing to return to England, and his hesitancy to move in one direction or the other. The question of acquiring property on Lake Chapala is raised again in a letter to Knud Merrild, one of the two Danish artists who had lived with the Lawrences on their New Mexican ranch, and who were now quartered in Los Angeles. In this letter, Lawrence says that he and Frieda have been sailing round the Lake to look at *haciendas,* but that they are afraid to buy because of a possible revolution. He adds in the same letter:

But I really hope that before long we may meet again, all of us, and try to make a life in common once more. If I can't stand Europe we'll come back to Mexico and spit on our hands and stick knives and revolvers in our belts . . . and have a place here . . . We have to be a few men with honor and fearlessness, and make a life together. There is nothing else, believe me.

54

The above passage illustrates Lawrence's ever-recurring desire to go with a few chosen friends to some remote spot, and to establish a utopia there.

Witter Bynner and "Spud" Johnson had taken rooms at the Hotel Arzapalo, but they customarily spent their evenings with Lawrence and Frieda. On Thursday and Sunday evenings there were band concerts in the plaza, where the Mexican girls walked round and round in an inner circle while the Mexican men walked round in an outer circle, in the opposite direction. On these occasions the Lawrences walked in the women's circle, while Bynner and Johnson walked in that of the men.

At Chapala Lawrence sat under a pepper tree, writing *The Plumed Serpent* in his familiar ten-cent copybooks. From time to time a wandering burro would approach him, sniff at him inquisitively, and then, when the strange man failed to respond, amble nonchalantly away. Perhaps because Lawrence was sensitive about his thinness, he never went swimming with the others in the whitish waters of the Lake. But Frieda enjoyed her swims until one day a large snake, lifting its head high above the surface near where she was standing, gave her an ugly fright.

The manager of the Arzapalo Hotel upset Lawrence considerably with his stories of bandits who had come down from the mountains and committed awful crimes in the town of Chapala. One night somebody broke a pane of glass in the door of Lawrence's bedroom. Presently in the darkness he saw, or thought he saw, a brown hand reach through the hole in the glass and slowly turn the key. By the time he had yelled and leaped out of bed the marauder, real or imaginary, had disappeared. Thenceforth Daniel, a brother of the servant Isabel, always slept across the doorway with a pistol at his side.

The boat trip referred to in Lawrence's letter to Knud Merrild was taken in a huge old *canoa* named *Esmeralda,* with a passenger list composed of Lawrence, Frieda, Bynner, Johnson, Idella Purnell (a poet who lived in Guadalajara and published a magazine called *Palms*), Idella's father, and Isabel the maid. The craft was manned by a Mexican "captain" and a couple of sailors, who punted it out from the shore while half the population of Chapala watched. In the middle of the lake a primitive sort of sail was hoisted. Then one of the sailors, whose work was finished for the present, began to sing and play a guitar.

When the group got tired of sailing they stopped and had a swim. By and by they landed on an island called the Isle of Scorpions. Here Lawrence bought a goat which the Mexicans, much to Frieda's disgust, slaughtered and skinned for food. After supper, while the Mexican sailor played his guitar, the whole group sang. Finally they all lay down to sleep—the men at one end of the *canoa,* the women at the other—underneath the flimsy canvas awning which was their only protection. In the middle of the night a furious wind arose, accompanied by a lashing rain. Bynner and Idella Purnell, as a result of the boat's tossing, became desperately ill. In the morning they were set ashore at an Indian village where they would be able to take the steamer back to Chapala. The others in the party sailed for three days more.

Soon after the momentous cruise Bynner had to go to the hospital in Guadalajara for a painful and fairly serious operation. During his convalescence Lawrence and Frieda were very kind. Lawrence, especially, spent hours showing Bynner how to make a silver necklace, and how to mend a worn *sarape.* Lawrence had, by the way, designed a number of *sarapes* and had them woven by Indians in one of the lakeside villages.

The sojourn at Chapala did not result in the purchase of a *hacienda*. Lawrence was still uncertain as to whether he preferred to live in America or in Europe. There was no indecision in the mind of Frieda, though. She wanted to go to England to see her children, and to Germany to see her aging mother. In July, presumably at her insistence, the Lawrences left Mexico, planning to return to England via New Orleans and New York. From the former city Lawrence wrote to Catherine Carswell:

Back in U.S.A.—regret Mexico—staying here a few days—a dead, steaming sort of place, a bit like Martin Chuzzlewit—dreary going up to New York by boat. The Mississippi is a vast and weary river that looks as if it had never wanted to start flowing. Expect to be in England before September.

On arriving in New York, Lawrence and Frieda discovered that it was impossible to book passage for England immediately. While waiting for something to turn up they sojourned briefly in New Jersey. This delay gave Lawrence a chance to change his mind, and to decide that Frieda, since she insisted on sailing now, would have to sail alone. He wrote to Knud Merrild:

I think I shall stay this side. I don't want to go; don't know why. I think, when Frieda has gone, I shall come to Los Angeles. We might like to spend the winter at Palm Springs or among the hills. Or we might go again to Mexico. And I should like to see you and Götzsche and have a talk about the future. If there was nothing else to do, we might take a donkey and go packing among the mountains. Or we might find some boat, some sailing ship that would take us to the islands.

The above excerpt suggests at least a temporary rejection,

by Lawrence, both of England and of his wife, in favor of a westward voyage with male companions. A week later, however, he writes to Middleton Murry that he has "a heavy feeling in his belly" when he thinks of his home and of his people back in England. Poor Lawrence, tortured constantly by indecision and remorse!

On August eighteenth Frieda sailed for Southampton on the *S. S. Orbita*, of the Royal Mail Steam Packet Line. Lawrence wrote to Middleton Murry and to Catherine Carswell asking them to look after her a bit in London. Then he went, by way of Buffalo—the girlhood home of Mabel Dodge Luhan—and Chicago, to California.

This is perhaps as good a place as any for a brief discussion of *The Plumed Serpent*, the novel of which Lawrence wrote the first draft while he and Frieda were living at Chapala, and which he intended to call by the name of the Aztec god, Quetzalcoatl. Of this book, in *Son of Woman*, Middleton Murry says: "*The Plumed Serpent* is absorbing both as a document and as an imaginative achievement. It is Lawrence's last effort at complete expression of himself in his fulness. . . . It is Lawrence's greatest work of 'art.' But," he adds, "the triumph of the 'artist' is the defeat of the prophet." In this, as in other matters, Murry disagrees with Catherine Carswell, who writes:

Surely here is the most ambitious and the most impressive novel of our generation. If any has been more faultless, which has possessed in the same degree the blazing virtue of potency? . . . So far from showing "disintegration" it creates. In it Lawrence's powers as a novelist are established and his thoughts as a man embodied to that extent that it would have assured him his place without further production.

Murry's opinion, on the contrary, appears to be reflected in the following statements by Hugh Kingsmill:

In comparison with *The Rainbow* and *Women in Love,* the up-rush from the dark unconscious has lost a good deal of its momentum in *The Plumed Serpent.* Lawrence was getting tired, and the effort to present himself as daemonic was becoming increasingly fatiguing. . . . Not so lush as *The Rainbow* and *Women in Love, The Plumed Serpent* is at least as preposterous, the difference in verisimilitude being only such as might exist between one of Tennyson's *Idylls of the King* rewritten in a madhouse by Dostoieffsky, and Rider Haggard's *She* transposed by Nietzsche into the style of *Also Sprach Zarathustra.*

No wonder H. T. Moore calls Kingsmill "Lawrence's cruellest biographer"!

The heroine of *The Plumed Serpent* is an Irish woman named Kate Leslie, who is in her early forties. Her first husband has divorced her, and her second has died. Her initial impressions of Mexico, like those of Lawrence himself, are of something evil, something cruel, something sinister. She is disgusted, as he was disgusted, by the spectacle of the bullfight, where: "Blindly and stupidly the bull ran at the rag, each time, and the toreadors skipped like fathipped girls showing off. Probably it needed skill and courage, but it looked silly." Presently, however, Kate becomes interested in the Aztec god, Quetzalcoatl, who is half bird and half serpent, and who represents the breath of life. She meets two Mexicans, Don Ramón and Don Cipriano, who plan, for political purposes, to revive the worship of Quetzalcoatl. Don Ramón poses as the incarnation of Quetzalcoatl, while Don Cipriano claims to be that of another Aztec god, Huitzilopochtli. Kate is persuaded to accept a metamorphosis into Malintzi, priestess of the peculiar cult. She even allows Don Ramón to marry her to Don Cipriano, with a ceremony in which she says: "This man is my rain from heaven," and Don Cipriano responds: "This woman is the earth to me." But Kate refuses, after the ceremony, to live with Don Cipriano as his wife. For a time he resigns himself, concentrating, with Don Ramón, on the propagation of the mystic religion. Later, when he seeks again to press himself upon her, Kate declares that she is sick and tired of the Aztec gods, of their latter-day impersonators, and of her own role as the priestess of their flimsy cult. In the end, though, when Don Cipriano returns triumphant from a series of bloody battles, she comes to him to be his wife forever, because, as she cries ecstatically, "You won't let me go!"

The Plumed Serpent is by no means as "preposterous" as Hugh Kingsmill would have us believe. Nor can one agree with Catherine Carswell in calling it "the most ambitious and the most impressive novel of our generation." She is right, however, in insisting that the novel possesses, to a high degree, "the blazing virtue of potency." *The Plumed Serpent* is rather long, and it has perhaps too much talk in it. But it is a powerful evocation of Mexico, past and present.

Merrild and Götzsche met Lawrence at Los Angeles, where the former was now employed by an architect, the latter by a motion picture studio. They drove him in "Lizzie" to Santa Monica, where he was installed at the Miramar Hotel. The Danes noticed that Lawrence was looking extremely seedy. Although he was not willing to submit to the will of Frieda, he seemed unable to get along for any length of time without her. Even after a visit to Santa Barbara he failed to express enthusiasm for the far-famed scenery and climate of southern California. Merrild and Götzsche were living temporarily in the home of an engineer named Harry R. Johnson, whose library they were decorating with frescoes. Lawrence wanted to help with the frescoes; the Danes, knowing that he lacked the necessary technical skill, used various pretexts to keep him out of the way. Thus he found himself wandering alone about the docks in San Pedro or in Wilmington, in search of a boat that he and his friends could buy and in which they could sail away on a golden voyage of adventure. In September he wrote to Spud Johnson that he was going to Lower California, or possibly to "the Pacific Isles." Fortunately for Lawrence's pocketbook, and also for his personal safety and that of his friends, he never found a suitable boat. He wrote to Middleton Murry that he had decided to travel down the west coast of Mexico with a Danish friend, looking for a place to live. They might be able to establish a ranch, and give the world "a new navel, a new centre."

The "Danish friend" was Götzsche, Lawrence having been unable to persuade Merrild to go back with him to Mexico. Merrild did not wish to become dependent upon Lawrence's emotional whims, now that Frieda was no longer there to provide an anchor to windward. Lawrence and Götzsche, leaving Los Angeles by train on September twenty-fifth, went by way of Palm Springs to Guaymas, a lovely Mexican resort on the Gulf of California. Lawrence admired the "strange and beautiful" country around Guaymas. It was full of wild duck, geese, and pelicans. A man there offered to give him six or eight acres of land on which to build a house. Yet Lawrence hung back. The place was just too lonely.

A letter Lawrence wrote to Witter Bynner at this time is filled with vivid description: "There is a blazing sun, a vast hot sky, big lonely inhuman green hills and mountains, a flat blazing littoral with a few palms, sometimes a dark blue sea which is not quite of this earth." He goes on to speak of buzzards thick as flies, and donkeys moving in a golden cloud of dust. Abandoned silver mines were hidden in the mountains. Dead dogs sometimes lay stretched in the middle of the market places. Many of the *haciendas* were owned and operated by Chinese, by whom Lawrence considered the coast to have been infested. He ended by saying that he and Götzsche, when they got to Mazatlan, would probably take a boat to Manzanillo, and go from there to Guadalajara.

The October sun was scorching, and the crawling trains would stop for hours, with no apparent pretext, at every God-forsaken village. Lawrence found the west coast wild and "hopeless." A cattle ranch they visited seemed "desolate" and "brutal." Götzsche became alarmed at his friend's depressed state of mind, which seemed to him at times to border on insanity. Yet Lawrence had unquestionably retained a certain grim sense of humor, as evidenced by the following paragraph from a letter that he wrote to Knud Merrild:

A circus follows us down the coast and the lions roar all night. The turkeys put their heads through the door—the doors are just wooden gates—and gobble at dawn. The people in the streets linger to look in and see how you're sleeping. The horse-riding lady from the circus has the next room, and stalks about with yards of bushy hair sticking out, rather fat inside a violent dressing-gown.

Finally, on October sixth, Lawrence and Götzsche reached Mazatlan. It was a lively seaport town, surrounded by luxuriant tropical vegetation. But, by night as well as by day, the heat was intolerable. Perhaps because of the heat, the fellow-sufferers abandoned their project to go farther down the coast, by boat, to Manzanillo. Instead they took a train eastward to Tepic, which was the railroad terminus and which, being situated at an altitude of three thousand feet, would at least be somewhat cooler. Tepic, however, seemed so desolate and lifeless that they decided to leave for Guadalajara immediately. After riding a bus as far as they could, they covered the remainder of the distance to the nearest railroad station on muleback.

Lawrence and Götzsche arrived in Guadalajara on the fifteenth of October. Having taken rooms at the Hotel García, off they went into the countryside, almost like Don Quixote and Sancho Panza, searching still for the elusive *hacienda!* Lawrence even risked a return to Lake Chapala where, only three months previously, he and Frieda had been so happy together. But alas! the Lake, like the Lac du Bourget in the famous poem of Lamartine, was not the same without Elvire. Lawrence told Götzsche, with tears in his eyes, that he no longer had the slightest desire to linger there.

Back in Guadalajara, Lawrence began, in fulfilment of his agreement with Mrs. M. L. Skinner, to rewrite her Australian novel, which she had originally entitled *The House of Ellis,* and which he now re-named *The Boy in the Bush.* On November fifteenth the job was finished, and the manuscript, which was to be published as a collaborative venture, dispatched to Curtis Brown. No doubt this resumption of creative activity did Lawrence a lot of good. The letters he wrote at this time to Mabel Dodge Luhan and Witter Bynner suggest a resurgence of his love for Mexico and of his love of life.

What of Frieda Lawrence all this time? In *Not I But The Wind* she writes:

So I went to England alone and had a little flat in Hampstead to see something of my children. It was winter and I wasn't a bit happy alone there and Lawrence was always cross when I had this longing for the children upon me; but there it was, though now I know he was right: they didn't want me any more, they were living their own lives. I felt lost without him.

Frieda wrote to Lawrence telling him that England was the place for him, and that she wanted him to come home. He did not do so at once, however. Could it be that knowing she wanted him gave him the necessary courage to remain away from her? At any rate, from his stronghold in Guadalajara, he wrote as follows to Catherine Carswell:

Mexico has a certain mystery of beauty for me, as if the gods were here. . . . I wish it could be that I could start a little centre —a ranch—where we could have our little adobe houses and make a life, and you could come, with Don and John Patrick.

Here it is again—the utopia complex! And Lawrence's pathetic indecision is once more expressed at the conclusion of this letter, where he hints that, after all, his destiny may be in Europe.

By November seventeenth, indeed, Lawrence and Götzsche had registered at the Hotel Monte Carlo in Mexico City. Lawrence had now made up his mind to go home; for, as he explained in a letter to Mrs. Skinner, it was necessary, since his wife refused to join him in Mexico, for him to join her in England. He wrote to Curtis Brown that he hoped to be in London on time for Christmas. And to Witter Bynner:

Mexico seems cold and dark after Jalisco. . . . I want to get a boat on, as soon as I can now, to England. God knows how long I shall stay there. This cold glowing morning in this city makes me think of it with repugnance. It was just nicely warm in Guadalajara. . . . Perhaps later we'll all meet and make a place in Jalisco. . . . This city doesn't feel right—feels like a criminal plotting his next rather mean crime. . . . *Hasta luego*.

Two days later, writing to Spud Johnson, Lawrence says: "I am off to Europe—*la malasuerte*. We sail, Götzsche and

I, on the *Toledo*, from Vera Cruz, on Thursday . . . and I get to Plymouth about 12 Decem." He states that a serious revolution is in the making. There is "no business doing," and the common people are "a bit brutal." Heaven has descended to earth, "with a red rag," and he himself is "the bull." (In politics, Lawrence is often extremely reactionary.) "I bought a *sarape* in the Volador," he remarks, "dark brown with big white stripes and *boca*—eleven *pesos*." Then the inevitable utopia: "I hope we shall all one day become quite nice people, and make a new spot on earth, more or less together." Lawrence's last letter from Mexico was addressed to Harriet Monroe, whom he told that he was "not very keen on going to Europe." It was four years, however, since he had left his native land to wander, by way of Sicily, India, Australia, and the United States, to Mexico. And when at last on November twenty-second he found himself aboard a vessel bound for England, his heart was wrung with an emotion difficult to analyze, but impossible to deny. There was a two-day stop in Havana. When the *Toledo* touched at Plymouth Lawrence disembarked; Götzsche went on to Hamburg, and from there to Denmark.

Lawrence's brief sojourn in London was not, unfortunately, a very happy one. Almost immediately he became jealous of Middleton Murry, who seemed to him to be excessively intimate with Frieda. At a certain tea party, when Frieda upbraided him in the presence of the other guests, he seized a poker, smashed the cups and saucers with it, and assured her that, if she ever spoke to him like that again, he would smash her head.

Then there was the famous "Last Supper" incident, which all of Lawrence's biographers have described at length. It occurred as the result of his inevitable desire to gather about him a group of chosen disciples, who would go back

65

with him to Taos, there to establish the community that he had always aspired to found. Seven of his closest friends, including Middleton Murry, the Carswells, Mary Cannan, and Dorothy Brett (an artist who had been a friend of Katherine Mansfield's) were invited to dine at the Café Royal. Since some of these people were by no means intimate with one another, Lawrence plied them, somewhat too liberally, with wine. When everyone had become sufficiently convivial he made a speech, in which he tried to explain what he was attempting to accomplish in the world, and invited them all to come to New Mexico to help him in the task. Under the influence of alcohol, every guest, with the exception of Mary Cannan, agreed. Murry went so far as to kiss Lawrence. "Do not betray me," Lawrence said. "I love you, Lorenzo," Murry answered, "but I won't promise not to betray you." Shortly after this Lawrence became sick and had to be taken home. In the morning he amiably confessed that he had made a fool of himself, adding that it behooved him, now that he had confessed it, to forget about it. When he and Frieda sailed for New York on the *Aquitania* on March 5, 1924, after a few weeks in Paris and Baden-Baden, their only companion was the artist **Dorothy Brett.**

TAOS II

THE LAWRENCES, accompanied by Dorothy Brett, their artist friend, arrived in Taos during the third week of March, 1924. In New York, where rain alternated with snow, they had been taken to dine and to the theatre by Lawrence's publisher, Thomas Seltzer. But Seltzer, who had suffered financial reverses, was unable to pay Lawrence more than a fraction of the royalties due him, and the latter refused to be mollified by his hospitality. Indeed, at a tea where he was graciously entertained, Lawrence became so refractory as to insist that art and literature were bosh, and that people were fools to pay any attention to them. In Chicago Harriet Monroe, the editor of *Poetry*, introduced the party to a group of writers. When they got to Taos they stayed for a few days at the "Big House" of Mabel Luhan, who happened to be away at the time. Mabel, as soon as she returned, immediately placed her two-story guest house at the disposal of the Lawrences, while "Brett," as everybody called her, was quartered in a small adobe one very near.

Brett was the daughter of Viscount Esher, and therefore entitled to be mentioned, on formal occasions, as "the Honourable Dorothy Brett." Since she was, unfortunately, very deaf, she made constant use of an old-fashioned ear-

trumpet to which she referred affectionately as "Toby."
Mabel's first impression of Brett, recorded eight years later,
runs like this:

She had pretty, pink, round cheeks and a childish expression.
Her long, thin shanks ended in large feet that turned out abrupt-
ly like the kind that children draw. She was an amusing and an
attractive grotesque, and her eyes were both hostile and ques-
tioning as she came slowly up to me, examining me, curious,
arrogant, and English.

Mabel's husband, Tony, was of course an Indian, and her
living room was often full of Indians. "These," she explained
to Brett, "are my relations."

Lawrence taught Brett to ride a horse. He sometimes
went riding with Mabel also. But Mabel received her greatest thrill when Lawrence allowed her to trim his beard.
"He sat meek and good like a little boy, a white towel tied
around his neck, and the red bits of hair fell around him on
the floor." In the evenings Lawrence, Frieda, Brett, and
Mabel often played mah jong, which was then a new game
Mabel had just imported from California.

Mabel was preparing her small "Pink House," which
stood in an alfalfa field, for the arrival of a friend named
Alice Sprague. Lawrence suggested that all of them set to
work to decorate it. Frieda painted a walnut chest of draw-
ers pale pink. Then she did its handles, which were carved
with bunches of grapes and leaves, in purple and emerald
green. Brett, on the lower half of the front door, designed
an apple tree, a serpent, and a brown-skinned Adam and
Eve. On the upper half of the door Lawrence placed his
emblem—a phoenix rising from its nest in flames. But this
phoenix was nothing compared with the masterpiece which
he created for the door of the outside toilet, and which

68

consisted of a mammoth sunflower with a green snake wrapped around its stem, surrounded by "a black butterfly as large as a plate, a white dove, a dark-brown bull-frog, and a rooster."

Once or twice a week Mabel took her friends to bathe in the hot springs, about fifteen miles from Taos, beside the Rio Grande. It was a deserted spot, where nobody was to be seen except an occasional shepherd tending his flock on the mountain-side. Hot water, "charged with radium," bubbled out of the sand to form a steaming pool, above which someone had built a little stone house. Mabel and Frieda and Brett would bathe first, while Tony built a fire on the ground outside. Sometimes the women thought they heard strange rumbling noises coming up from the distant depths of the earth. They always left the pool, rejuvenated, after five minutes, for a longer period sapped one's strength. When Tony and Lawrence bathed, the contrast between their bodies was very striking. While Tony was sturdily built and had brown skin, Lawrence was slender and his skin was white. But in spite of his frailty there was a sort of nervous toughness about him. Mabel, seeing him standing by the fire clad only in his bathing trunks and with his great red beard, thought that he resembled John the Baptist.

One day when Frieda, Lawrence, and Brett were bathing at the hot springs they were accompanied by the actress Ida Rauh, who, with her young son, was also visiting Mabel Dodge Luhan. Lawrence asked her what kind of plays she liked best, and she replied: "Stories from the Bible." When Lawrence asked her if she knew the story of David's wife, Michal, she said no. So he told her how, after David came from the wars, Michal said that she would

69

never live with him again, and never did. "I'll write a play about it for you," said Lawrence. This was the genesis of his play, *David*.

As might have been expected, it wasn't long before tensions developed among Mabel and Brett and Frieda Lawrence. One evening when Mabel had invited the Lawrences and Brett to supper at "the Big House," and they all had declined, she entered the Lawrences' guest house to find Brett eating supper there with *them*. But the incident is graphically described, in *Lawrence and Brett*, by Brett herself:

In she walks, without speaking or looking at us, and sits down on the day-bed. Not a word is spoken by any of us. She leans back, silent, like a stone monument. . . . Frieda's eyes are blazing, and you Lawrence look down at your plate, entirely withdrawn. . . . At last, as suddenly as she came, she gets up and goes. Frieda gives a nervous giggle, but you are cold with anger. . . . I feel an undercurrent of emotional strain.

Mabel was annoyed by Brett's ear-trumpet, which always seemed to be spying on her and Lawrence. Lawrence and Frieda, perceiving her uneasiness, apologized for Brett, Lawrence arguing that her deafness made her quite innocuous, and Frieda insisting that she was, after all, only a sort of typist for Lawrence, and hence hardly to be reckoned with. When Mabel allowed Brett to cut her hair, the shears slipped and nicked the tip of Mabel's ear. Mabel felt sure that Brett had tried, consciously or unconsciously, to mutilate her ear because she herself was deaf! But in spite of the emotional tension Lawrence wrote to Harriet Monroe:

We find Taos very pleasant again . . . and the raging spirits somewhat soothed. My wife just calming down after the depressing swirl of Europe, and Dorothy Brett blissfully happy on an old horse. . . . I must say I am glad to be out here in the southwest of America—there is the pristine something, unbroken, unbreakable . . . for which I thank whatever gods there be.

Among the rather eccentric people that Mabel entertained from time to time was Jaime, a swarthy young Spaniard with whom she liked to discuss psychoanalysis, and who went about informing people that he was writing a book. Jaime was addicted to blue berets, rope-soled sandals, and bell-bottom trousers. He was fond of stripping to the waist and flexing his biceps in the presence of the ladies, a habit which led Lawrence to predict that some day the man would forget himself so far as to remove not only his shirt but his trousers also. One day Mabel took her friends to an Indian dance at the pueblo of Santo Domingo. There Jaime, having bought a blue and white striped *sarape,* threw it over his shoulder and announced that he was going to walk, just as he was, to California. They didn't believe him until they saw him far away in the desert, headed west.

A short distance across the desert from Mabel's Big House stood one of the many Penitente *moradas,* or chapels, which are found in Taos Valley. Leaning against the windowless adobe structure were several of the heavy wooden crosses that the Penitentes drag at night, during the Lenten season, along the road called "Calvary." At such times some of them beat themselves with cactus whips, while one plays eerie tunes on a primitive wooden flute. Most of Mabel's guests were fascinated by the chants and cries that sometimes came at night from the *morada.* But Lawrence would close his windows in order not to hear them. He did not like the Penitentes.

The Indians, however, were another matter. Lawrence liked them, and, in general, got along with them very well. He particularly enjoyed it when a number of them were

71

invited to Mabel's house in the evening for a dance. There would be a blazing fire on the hearth. The Indians would dress in moccasins, loin-cloths, and beaded jackets, with headdresses made of feathers and with bells attached to their knees. The drum would pound, and the Indians would dance their measured tread around the room. Soon the air would be filled with noise, heat, and excitement. Lawrence himself, after a while, would be drawn into the dance, to go treading round and round with an Indian on either side of him. This was really amazing, for Lawrence could rarely be induced to dance with white people. He thought that the one-step was indecent.

It will be recalled that the Lawrences and their Danish friends had spent the winter of 1922-23 at Mabel's Del Monte Ranch, seventeen miles from Taos and nearly two thousand feet higher, at an altitude between eight and nine thousand feet. Mabel now offered to give a part of the ranch, thenceforth known as Kiowa, to Lawrence. But Lawrence, ever wary of accepting gifts, declined. Then Mabel offered the ranch to Frieda, who accepted it. Lawrence insisted, however, on repaying Mabel by making her a present of the manuscript of *Sons and Lovers*. Mabel, according to Witter Bynner, later gave the manuscript to Dr. Brill, her psychoanalyst, who in turn sold it.

Lawrence, feeling that things would be more peaceful at Kiowa Ranch, proposed that he and Frieda and Brett move up there to spend the summer. When they arrived on a tour of inspection they found the cabins in a very dilapidated state. One of them seemed habitable. The second was hardly big enough to hold a bed. And the third appeared to be full of cow-dung. But the view was splendid, and Mabel assured them that they could, with the help of a few Indians, put the place in order. On the fifth of May, with three horses loaned by Mabel, they moved up to the ranch. Lawrence and Frieda would live in the largest cabin, which had a living room, two bedrooms, and a kitchen. Brett would have the smallest one, an adobe with a shingle roof. And the medium-sized one, after it had been repaired, would be kept as a sort of guest house, where Mabel could come and stay whenever she liked.

The amount of work to be done on the ranch, even with the Indians' help, was really staggering. The cabins had to be repaired, the fences mended, the well cleaned out, and a ditch dug for irrigation. Brett did more than her share. Frieda cooked tremendous meals for the toilers. Lawrence, out of the little money he had left, bought a cow named Susan, a cock named Moses, and a flock of hens. While Lawrence and Frieda and Brett were settling in at the ranch, the Indians camped above them among the pines, where Tony and Mabel also had their tepee.

Mabel, now and then, would drive down to Taos for fresh supplies. Brett chopped wood and carried water. Frieda, in the intervals between cooking, would stretch out on her bed and smoke a cigarette. Lawrence and Brett would sometimes join in singing old English or Scottish ballads. Or they would drop in at the neighboring cabin of Bill and Rachel Hawk. Lawrence never asked the Indians, who called him "Red Fox," to do anything he wasn't willing to do himself, and he fed them plentifully. They seemed to like him, and he liked them in return, at least until someone told him that they were laughing at him behind his back.

Brett, to form the arch of the fireplace in the big cabin, picked up half of the steel rim of an old wagon wheel. One of the Indians flattened it a bit, it was set in place, and then the adobe was molded over it. On either side of the fireplace Lawrence placed large flat stones which, when covered with cement, made perfect seats. While he labored, Brett stood beside him like a handmaiden, passing him whatever tool he needed. She wore a wide-brimmed sombrero, and corduroy trousers tucked into her high boots. Into one high boot she had also thrust a long-bladed stiletto, for Brett was always fond of knives.

Lawrence had learned that Middleton Murry was about to marry Violet Le Maistre. He wrote to congratulate him, and then went on:

I think by the end of next week the houses will be done. There's a two-room cabin where Mabel can come when she likes, and a one-roomer for Brett. . . . England is as unreal as a book one read long ago. . . . Often . . . it is trying—and one has to bear up hard against it. Then the altitude about 8,600 ft. tells on one for a time. The sun is setting and the pines are red, the Indians are just starting drumming. All good luck to you.

Two days later he wrote to Catherine Carswell:

I think we shall stay till October, then go down to Mexico, where I must work at my novel *The Plumed Serpent*. At present I don't write—don't want to—don't care. Things are all far away. I haven't seen a newspaper for two months, and can't bear to think of one. The world is as it is. I am as I am. We don't fit very well.

In the evening, while the oil lamp glimmered, strange discussions used to occur. According to Brett, Lawrence, in one of his condemnatory moods, declared that St. Francis of Assisi was "disgusting" and "loathsome" when he kissed a leper and ate dirt. Of James Joyce's *Ulysses* he remarked: "The last part of it is the dirtiest, most indecent, obscene thing ever written. . . . It is filthy." He hated Frazer, author of *The Golden Bough,* for writing from an armchair, "never having seen an Indian or a tiger or known anything." He

74

doubted if James Fenimore Cooper had ever seen an Indian.

Lawrence wrote to London, to his publisher Martin Secker, asking him for six-months' subscriptions to a couple of popular magazines, and for some books, old or new, to read at the ranch. When Secker sent him E. M. Forster's splendid novel, *A Passage to India,* he somewhat condescendingly replied: "It's good, but makes one wish a bomb would fall and end everything. Life is more interesting in its undercurrents than in its obvious; and E. M. does see people, people, and nothing but people, *ad nauseam.*"

Meanwhile the work continued as before. Lawrence was up each day at five. He would hunt for Susan, the black cow, and scold her for hiding in the woods. He built cupboards and painted woodwork. He helped Brett paint and entertained his friends. And, in addition to all of these activities, he had begun again to write. As for Frieda: "I made our own butter in a little glass churn," she writes, "and the chickens flourished on the buttermilk, and so did we in this healthy life. We made our own bread in the Indian oven outside, black bread and white, and cakes." Wild raspberries grew in the canyon, but Frieda was afraid to pick them because of bears.

Often in the morning Lawrence, dressed in his corduroy pants, blue shirt, and big straw hat, wandered off into the woods to work on *St. Mawr,* his newest novel. With his fountain pen and his copybook he sat and leaned against the trunk of a tree, lost in the strange world of his imagining. When Brett, coming up to fetch him for dinner, roused him suddenly, he sometimes got angry and lashed out at her.

The heroine of *St. Mawr* is Lou Witt, a twenty-five-year-old American girl. She is the wife of Rico Carrington, a wealthy young Australian whom she met in Rome and married in Paris. They live in London, where Rico paints, Lou entertains, and each gets on the other's nerves. Meanwhile Lou's mother, Mrs. Witt, looks on sardonically. Lou becomes infatuated with a handsome stallion named St. Mawr and buys him, along with his Welsh groom Lewis, "for Rico." Rico, riding St. Mawr in Rotten Row, fails to master the animal, and is requested not to ride him there again. Lou and Rico and Mrs. Witt take a house in Shropshire for the summer. Rico fits into the community, but Mrs. Witt despises it, and the two are at swords' points. When St. Mawr crushes Rico's ankle and kicks a friend of his in the face, Rico sells him to an Englishwoman who plans to geld him. But Mrs. Witt and Lewis take St. Mawr and another horse and ride away to Oxfordshire. Presently Lou, having left her husband, meets her mother and Lewis in London. The three of them, together with St. Mawr and a Mexican groom named Phoenix, embark at Southampton for Galveston, Texas. In Havana Mrs. Witt and Lou look on disgustedly at the drinking of some American tourists. Even when they reach their ranch in Texas, they are not at ease. Leaving St. Mawr and Lewis there, they move on to Santa Fe, New Mexico. Phoenix is happy now, but they are not. Lou buys a mountain ranch for twelve hundred dollars. She and her mother and Phoenix will live there together, away from the importunities of other men and women. . . .

St. Mawr was originally published in the same volume with "The Princess," a tale written in 1924, describing the adventures of an unmarried woman from Boston who has an affair, in the mountains of New Mexico, with a rancher of Spanish descent, but remains sexually frigid.

Mabel, wishing to contribute something to Lawrence's cabin at the ranch, made him a huge armchair. It had as its covering a Navajo blanket, held in place with great, brass-headed nails. Mabel hoped that Lawrence would sit in it to do his writing. When it was finished she had it lifted into a wagon and driven up to the ranch. Alas! the mighty chair failed to impress Lawrence, who called it "The Iron Maiden," and refused to sit in it.

Porcupines were eating bands of bark around the trees at Lawrence's ranch. When Mabel and Tony went up to visit, the latter immediately took his gun and went out to hunt the pernicious animals. Presently a shot rang out, and a little later Tony appeared with a dead porcupine. Lawrence was furious. "I don't want any shooting here!" he cried. "I like porcupines!" Tony tried to explain that the trees were being ruined, but Lawrence wouldn't listen. Becoming quite proprietary, he intimated that Tony, unless he would behave in accordance with his wishes, might as well leave.

Lawrence's reaction to the shooting of the porcupine made Mabel, as she informs us in *Lorenzo in Taos*, extremely angry. Flouncing out of her cabin, she climbed to the place where Tony and his Indian friends had pitched their camp. Then she sent for Lawrence. Tony, who disliked emotional scenes, left immediately. Mabel's messenger soon returned with the news that Lawrence had said: "If Mabel wants to see me, she can come down here." At this, striding down to the cabin where Lawrence and Frieda and Brett were washing the breakfast dishes, Mabel announced that she wanted to speak to Lawrence alone. Quietly he followed her over to the cabin where she had been staying. When the door was shut behind them, Mabel flung herself on the bed and wept. Lawrence sat and watched helplessly. By and by, while Mabel continued to weep, Frieda opened the door, took a look inside, and then went away leaving the door open. From time to time other people, walking past, looked in. Mabel enjoyed all this immensely. "I feel wonderful!" she exclaimed as she dried her tears. It seemed to her that she had made a precious "gift" to Lawrence on that day.

Frieda was often jealous of Mabel, and Mabel was often jealous of Brett. Lawrence would scold Mabel for being unkind to Brett, and he scolded Brett for not having enough respect for Frieda. All this resulted in tears and headaches for everyone concerned.

Lawrence had a colored print of *The Man with the Sunflower*. One day he amused himself by painting a copy of it. Both Mabel and Brett felt the painting to be an emblem of himself, and both coveted it. Mabel insisted that Lawrence had said she could have it. But, as it lay beside her on a table, Brett took it away and hid it. Mabel discovered where it was hidden and regained possession of it at once. Brett snatched it away from her. Poor Lawrence, who came in just then, tried in vain to make peace between the two women. Mabel pursued Brett round and round the house, until she caught her and seized the painting, to keep it always.

One Saturday afternoon Lawrence, Frieda, Brett, Mabel, and Tony took their horses and rode up into the mountains behind Arroyo Seco to see the famous Indian ceremonial cave. It was a hard ride, and Lawrence, at the end, was white and panting. But the cave was beautiful. It seemed immensely high, and over its mouth poured the glistening curtain of a waterfall. The cave was to reappear later in Lawrence's story, "The Woman Who Rode Away." The heroine of this story, who is never named, is an American woman in her early thirties. She is married to a Dutchman, twenty years older than herself, who owns a silver mine

78

in the Mexican state of Chihuahua. She does not love her
husband, and although they have two children, doesn't
seem much interested in them. Instead, she keeps brooding
about the distant mountains, and about the strange Chil-
chui Indians who are said to live in them. One day when
her husband is away on business she prepares some food,
mounts her horse, and, after placing her children in charge
of the servants, rides off into the hills. Higher and higher
she rides, stopping only to eat and to sleep, until on the
third day she is confronted by three Indians. When she
has explained to one of these Indians, who is able to understand Spanish, that she wishes to meet his people, they
take her reluctantly to their pueblo village and present her
to their aged *cacique,* or chief. The *cacique,* after hearing
her story, gives her food to eat, water in which to bathe,
fresh robes, and a little house and garden in an enclosure
whose gate is securely fastened. Here she lives, half drugged,
for weeks and months, until winter comes. Finally, at the
winter solstice, she is carried up to the ceremonial cave,
whose gaping mouth is covered by a frozen waterfall. She
is told that white men have stolen the sun from Indian
men, and that white women have stolen the moon from
Indian women. In order that Indian men may recover the
sun, and in order that Indian women may recover the moon,
she must be offered as a human sacrifice. Some Indians
seize her and lay her body on a large, flat stone. The sun
is setting:

When the red sun was about to sink, he would shine full through
the shaft of ice deep into the hollow of the cave, to the inner-
most. . . . She understood now that this was what the men were
waiting for. The black eyes of the aged *cacique* were fixed like
black mirrors on the sun. . . . In absolute motionlessness he
watched until the red sun should send his ray through the

column of ice. Then the old man would strike, and strike home, accomplish the sacrifice and achieve the power.

And thus the story ends!

Among Mabel's eccentric importations was Clarence, a youth as fair as Jaime had been dark. His hands and arms were covered with Indian silver jewelry, when he first arrived in Taos, and his most precious possession was a tiny, crystal rabbit. Lawrence, strange to relate, liked Clarence, or perhaps felt sorry for him. And Clarence stood in awe of Lawrence. He even sought to please him by wearing a red velvet Navajo jacket, with large silver buttons!

As time went on, Mabel's visits to the ranch became less frequent. She and Alice Sprague and Clarence "played around" together in Taos. Alice Sprague was living in the "Pink House" that stood in Mabel's alfalfa field. Feeling insecure at night, she always had someone prop a log against the *outside* of the door after she had gone to bed. Nobody ever disillusioned her as to the efficacy of this system of defense. Alice Sprague considered Mabel to be a dynamic woman, Clarence a darling boy, and Lawrence, of course, a genius. Whenever some angry outburst smashed the serenity of the group, she merely sat and sewed, a sweet smile hovering on her lips.

One Saturday evening Mabel invited Lawrence and Frieda and Brett to dinner at the "Big House." Two other guests were present—George Creel, husband of Blanche Bates, the actress, and a second gentleman who was Blanche Bates' leading man of the moment. Creel was eager to meet Lawrence, and wanted to give him letters of introduction to some people who could help him when he went to Mexico. But Lawrence, perhaps because he felt abashed in the presence of these handsome, well-dressed men, was almost boorish. He insisted on sitting with Frieda and Clarence at the far end of the table, making no attempt to converse with the other guests. When Mabel and the two strangers began to talk about the good times they had had together in New York, he became enraged. At the end of the meal he and Clarence, instead of going with the others into the living room, bolted through the kitchen and out of the house! It was over an hour before he returned to join the group. And even then, when Frieda told him that Mr. Creel would be glad to give him letters to friends in Mexico City, he retorted angrily that he had no need of letters from anyone. In a little while Creel and his friend departed, still smiling and still urbane.

On another occasion the Lawrences were staying, as before, at Mabel's place in Taos. Ordinarily, writes Mabel, very little drinking went on there, but on this particular evening several members of the group had been sampling a mixture of moonshine whiskey and ginger ale. Clarence, turning on the victrola in the studio, began to dance with Frieda. "Oh!" Alice Sprague exclaimed. "Isn't that a *picture?* They dance so beautifully together! That beautiful woman and that tall, lovely boy!" At this, Lawrence, who almost never danced, seized Mabel and set out clumsily but rapidly in pursuit of the other couple. Brett, with her brass ear-trumpet, trailed along behind. Lawrence and Mabel bumped into Clarence and Frieda as often and as hard as possible. These two, who were physically unmatched, seemed determined to destroy the physical harmony that existed between the other two.

The strange events that followed are described in various ways in the accounts of Mabel, of Frieda, and of Brett. It appears that Clarence and Frieda, leaving the studio, went out into the darkness together. Lawrence excused himself and returned to the guest house to go to bed. As for Tony

and Mabel, they soon retired to their sleeping porch up-
stairs in the Big House. But Mabel, when everything was
quiet, slipped down the stairs and out of the house to look
for Frieda and Clarence. Tony called her back. She did not
come. Tony rushed outside, jumped into his car, and went
to spend the night with his fellow-Indians at the Taos
Pueblo. On the following morning, after listening to the
pleas of Clarence, he consented to come home again.

Clarence now told Mabel that Lawrence had ruined
Frieda's life, and that he was plotting to ruin hers as well.
He even accosted Lawrence personally, accusing him of
evil purposes. Finally Tony drove the Lawrences, at their
own request, back to Kiowa Ranch. By and by, however,
Clarence began to feel sorry for the injustice he had done
to Lawrence. With his own hands he made a pine chest,
smoothed it, lacquered it, and sent it up to him. He gave
him also the object he cherished more than anything else—
his crystal rabbit.

Outside the Lawrences' cabin at Kiowa stood an Indian
oven, made of adobe and shaped like a beehive. Inside this
oven, when he wished to bake some bread, Lawrence
burned wood for half an hour. Then he raked the ashes
out, and swabbed the oven clean with a damp cloth on a
stick. He used a long, flat shovel to place the risen dough
inside the oven. And finally he sealed the oven door with
a board held in place by a heavy stone. After that, he had
only to sit and wait for the bread to bake. It was always
delicious.

One morning Lawrence, for the first time, spit blood.
Frieda was frightened; Brett pretended not to see. After
lunch, the latter informs us, Lawrence went to bed and
remained there until the following day. On learning that
Frieda had sent for a doctor he was beside himself with

rage. "How dare you!" he cried. And he hurled an iron egg-ring at his wife, missing her head by a fraction of an inch. "You *know* I dislike doctors," he went on. "You *know* I wouldn't have him or you wouldn't have sent for him behind my back!" Frieda tried to explain to Lawrence that no harm would be done if his illness wasn't serious, and that if it was serious the doctor could help him. He was still fuming helplessly when the doctor finally arrived. When his ailment was diagnosed as bronchial trouble, which a mustard plaster would relieve, he relaxed and smiled, and everyone felt better.

Frieda already rode a handsome horse, Azul. Lawrence, while still convalescing, bought a black horse named Aaron for himself, and a bay named Ambrose for Brett. He could hardly force himself to remain in bed while fresh bread was baked by Frieda and Brett and Spud Johnson, instead of by himself. As soon as he felt better they all went riding, and Lawrence scolded Frieda for falling off her horse.

In August Mabel drove Lawrence and Frieda to Arizona to see the Snake Dance of the Hopi Indians. On his return Lawrence wrote to Middleton Murry as follows:

That trip to the Hopi country was interesting, but tiring, so far in a motor car. The Navajo country is very attractive—all wild, with great red cliffs bluffing up. Good country to ride through, one day. The Navajos themselves real wild nomads; alas, they speak practically no English, and no Spanish. But strange, the intense religious life they keep up, in those round huts. This animistic religion is the only live one, ours is a corpse of a religion.

At the same time Lawrence wrote to Spud Johnson a very much longer letter, in which he bitterly derided the Hopi Indians, their country, their villages, and their Snake Dance:

The Hopi country is some forty miles across, and three stale

mesas jut up in its desert. The dance was on the last *mesa* . . .
in Hotevilla. . . . Hotevilla is a scrap of a place with a *plaza* no
bigger than a fair-sized back-yard. . . . A mile from the village
was improvised the official camping ground, like a corral with
hundreds of black motor cars. Across the deathgrey desert, bump
and lurch, came strings of more black cars, like a funeral *cortège*.
Till everybody had come—about three thousand bodies.

Lawrence goes on to ridicule the hundreds of "American
women in pants," who watched the dance from rooftops,
from windows, and from the ground surrounding the *plaza*.
Then he expresses his contempt for the dance itself, with
its grey or black daubed "priests," its hollow muttering,
and its lack of drums and pageantry. For a little while the
Indians hopped about with snakes between their teeth.
Then the snakes, like "wet silk stockings," were gathered
up and "let to wriggle all together for a minute in meal,
corn-meal, that the women of the pueblo had laid down on
the sand of the *plaza*." At last two priests picked the snakes
up and carried them off to set them free among the rocks.
Towards the end of the letter Lawrence writes:

The south-west is the great playground of the white American.
The desert isn't good for anything else. And the Indian, with
his long hair and bits of pottery and clumsy home-made trinkets,
he's a wonderful live toy to play with.

This same event is described by Lawrence in an article
called "The Hopi Snake Dance," which first appeared in
the *Adelphi* magazine, and was subsequently included in
Mornings in Mexico. In his article Lawrence describes the
dance at much greater length, of course, than in his letter
to Spud Johnson. Furthermore he adds considerable material on the religion of the Indians. And finally, which is
most important of all, he writes in an entirely different
tone. The note of derision, of ridicule, and of contempt is

almost wholly lacking from his article. "Amid all its crudity," he remarks, "and the sensationalism which comes chiefly out of the crowd's desire for thrills, one cannot help pausing in reverence before the delicate, anointed bravery of the snake-priests . . . with the snakes." Even of the spectators he is tolerant: "It is a good-humoured, very decent crowd, ready to respect any sort of feelings." How is one to explain this change in tone? Was Lawrence being sincere in the Johnson letter, and "giving the public what it wanted" in his article? Or had his estimate of the Hopi Snake Dance actually altered by the time he was ready to write for publication? As he himself would have said, *Quién sabe?* At all events Middleton Murry, who was editing the *Adelphi*, liked the article, for in his *Reminiscences* he calls it "an essay full of . . . delicate and spontaneous imaginative sympathy."

After Lawrence had returned from the Hopi Snake Dance, he and Brett and Rachel Hawk rode up to the peak of Lobo Mountain, where he had never been. Back again at the ranch he got angry at a brooding hen, and chopped her head off. "After supper," writes Brett, "we pluck her, singing old Scotch songs." Lawrence received word that his father had died on September tenth. One evening, in a bitter mood, he sat denouncing everyone for treachery and betrayal, and spitting into the fire. He no longer received letters from Mabel, for someone had told her he had branded her as "dangerous and destructive." After his outbursts Lawrence, to relieve his feelings, would fetch his little bag of threads and needles, and proceed, with incredible neatness, to turn the frayed cuffs of his shirt.

But Lawrence was anxious to be on the move again. Old Mexico, where he had already experienced some interesting adventures, was calling to him. He felt that he had to be

85

there in order to complete his novel, *The Plumed Serpent.*
On October eighth he wrote to Catherine Carswell:

We are packing up to leave here. . . . If the roads are passable,
we shall go down to Taos on Saturday, stay a day or two, then
go down to Mexico City. My spirit always wants to go south.
Perhaps one feels a bit of hope down there. . . . Brett will go
down with us. But if we take a house, she must take a little place
of her own. Not to be too close. . . . By being careful we manage
to have two thousand dollars to go to Mexico with. . . . The
house is half dismantled; we are fastening the place up and leaving
it.

When the packing was finished Lawrence closed the cabins.
Mabel came to fetch the trio in her car. And after waving
goodbye to the horses they drove off down the mountain,
towards Taos and Santa Fe.

OAXACA

In October, 1924, Lawrence, Frieda, and Brett visited the Mexican Consulate in El Paso to obtain their passport visas. The wrath of Frieda was aroused when the Mexican officials took her for Lawrence's mother, and Brett for his wife. The train for Mexico City was full of soldiers, supposed to protect them against the bandits who had been more or less rampant since the revolution. At every station platform the travelers were besieged by scores of black-haired women in earrings and *rebozos,* eager to sell them tropical fruits and other delicacies. Occasionally, in the course of the journey, Lawrence and Frieda quarreled. When Brett took Lawrence's part, Frieda became of course more furious than ever. They arrived in Mexico City after midnight, four hours late.

The party spent the night at the Hotel Regis, then one of Mexico City's most luxurious hotels; but in the morning, at Lawrence's insistence, they moved to the much less pretentious Monte Carlo, where they had stayed the previous year. Before long Lawrence began to receive invitations to receptions, teas, and luncheons. The P.E.N. Club gave a banquet in his honor one evening, at the Café Oriental. Lawrence didn't want to go, but Frieda and Brett insisted. At the banquet he was called upon, for the first and last time in his life, to make a speech. When he got home the women asked him on what subject he had addressed the group of writers. "I tried to explain to them," said Lawrence, "that it is less important for us to be artists than it is for us to be men. But of course they didn't understand. I was just another voice crying in the wilderness."

While in the capital the party attended a luncheon at which Frieda sat next to Mr. W. Somerset Maugham. Of this meeting she has written:

I felt sorry for Maugham; he seemed to me an unhappy and acid man, who got no fun out of living. . . . He could not accept the narrow social world and yet he didn't believe in a wider human one. . . . When I met other writers, then I knew without knowing (*sic*) how altogether different Lawrence was. They may have been good writers, but Lawrence was a genius.

The above passage, though a gratifying revelation of Frieda's respect for her husband as an artist, is manifestly unfair to Somerset Maugham. It was, I believe, a sense of his own inferiority to Maugham, in certain respects, that induced Lawrence to write, in a letter to Curtis Brown: "We met _____ _____ in Mexico City. He hates it here: has gone to Yucatan. He'll hate it there. I didn't like him." What was the point of dissension between D. H. Lawrence and Somerset Maugham? Lawrence, in spite of his intense convictions and his brilliant mind, never attained perfection as a fictional craftsman. But Maugham, without preaching any particular philosophy of life, delighted thousands with his sense of style, his talent for composition, and his flair for drama. Perhaps his popularity, rather than his personality, irritated Lawrence. Who can say? At any rate it is clear to-day that both writers deserve our respect and admiration, though for entirely different reasons.

It was cold and rainy in Mexico City, with an overtone

of dreariness that made Lawrence feel depressed. Frieda took to her bed with influenza. When Lawrence, with Brett, visited the National Museum, and a guard there ordered him to remove his hat, he vowed that he would never enter the Museum again. Lawrence and Brett went also to the Shrine of the Virgin of Guadalupe. Finally Lawrence himself had influenza, or "grippe," as he called it in a letter to Mabel Dodge Luhan. As soon as he got better he was anxious to leave Mexico City for the south at the earliest possible moment.

Seven months previously, on March 3, 1924, Lawrence had written to Witter Bynner from England saying that he wanted to visit Oaxaca. The British Vice-Consul in Mexico City had a brother who was a priest in that city, and who would, the Vice-Consul felt sure, be happy to help the Lawrences find a house there. Lawrence, who had been sorely tried by the altitude of nearly nine thousand feet at his ranch in New Mexico, expected that the climate of Oaxaca, so far south and only five thousand feet above sea level, would do him good. He and Frieda and Brett took the train one November morning at seven o'clock. On their left, as they journeyed south, they could see the two snow-capped volcanoes, Popocatepetl and Ixtaccihuatl. Lawrence, peering from the window, gnawed at his beard excitedly. At Esperanza they changed trains for Tehuacan, where they passed the night. The following morning they began the long, long journey through tropical forests and rocky canyons toward Oaxaca. As before, their train carried scores of soldiers to protect the passengers and freight from bandits. When finally they entered the long, green, lovely valley of Oaxaca it was growing dark. They proceeded in a mule-drawn tram from the railway station to the Hotel Francia. The proprietress of the hotel warned her guests, who were quartered on the ground floor, to put their luggage as far as possible from the windows, since otherwise their possessions might be stolen by thieves using long poles with hooks at the end.

Lawrence wrote Curtis Brown, his London literary agent, that Oaxaca was full of sunshine and roses, and that he thought he would rent a house in which to stay for a month or two. To his friend Middleton Murry he wrote of Oaxaca: "It's not far from both coasts, but there's no railway. You can ride in four or five days either to the Pacific or the Atlantic—if you don't get shot."

While Brett stayed on at the Hotel Francia, the Lawrences took the house found for them by the priest to whom they had a letter of introduction, at Avenida Pino Suárez 43. It was unfurnished, but various people to whom Lawrence had letters of introduction loaned tables, chairs, and beds. On the eighteenth of November they were able to move in. The house was blessed with a shady, red-tiled patio, smelling of resin, coffee, leaves, and sunburned earth. In the garden were orange trees and banana trees. From one of these the two green parrots used to mimic the voice of someone calling *"Perro! Perro! Perro!"* Then they would mimic, with infinite sarcasm, the barking of the *perro* himself, a fat little curly white dog named Corasmín.

With the Lawrences' house went an exasperating yet likable Mexican *mozo* named Rosalino. Unlike the average Zapotec Indian, who resembled the straight, sharp knife of black obsidian brought forth in childbirth by an Aztec goddess, Rosalino was softer, shyer, not so male. He was unable to carry anything very heavy, since he had been severely beaten for refusing to be a soldier in the army of the revolutionists. For two dollars a month he swept and sprinkled the patio, sleeping at night on a wooden bench in the entry of the house. When he retired at night the only preparation he made was to remove his sandals—his *huaraches*. Rosalino was a genius at bargaining in the market and loved to do it. Occasionally, becoming homesick for his village in the hills, he would threaten to leave, but at the last moment he would always change his mind.

Brett loved the covered market, where they went on Saturdays. "It is dark," she writes, "with great splashes of sunlight . . . here and there. There are flowers; masses and masses of flowers; clean, glistening vegetables and fruit; gorgeous *sarapes* . . . baskets. Color, color everywhere!" But the stench of the *huaraches*, or Mexican sandals, was almost too much for Brett. And one market day somebody stole her ear-trumpet, so that she had to have a local tinsmith improvise one until she could get another from England.

Sometimes, when Lawrence wandered about the town, the Indians would call *"Cristo! Cristo!"* after him. And indeed, with his ascetic pallor and his piercing eyes, he must have resembled a red-bearded Christ. One day an Indian woman followed Lawrence home with four ducks which she insisted on selling to him. In order to be rid of her Lawrence bought the ducks, and Rosalino obligingly dug a pond for them in the garden. Lawrence rewarded him with a new *sarape* to keep him warm when he slept at night on his wooden bench by the big front door. He also began to teach him to read and write. Rosalino imitated his master by taking a bath on Saturday night, and donned a clean and gaudy shirt on Sunday morning. He kept begging Lawrence to take him with him when he returned to London.

Lawrence devoted the mornings to his work on the revision of *The Plumed Serpent*, while Brett typed for him. Frequently he would be invited to dine by one or another of

91

the American families in Oaxaca. Ordinarily he would accept, but only with the understanding that the meal be served on time. He was willing to dine at seven or at nine— the hour made no difference—but he didn't like to wait. Lawrence had become enough of a personage, even in remote Oaxaca, to impose his will. This is further indicated by the following incident related by Frieda:

I went to the market with the *mozo* and one day he showed me in the square, in one of the bookshops, an undeniable caricature of Lawrence, and he watched my face to see how I would take it. I was thrilled! To find in this wild place, with its . . . undiluted Mexican tribes, anything so civilized as a caricature of Lawrence was fun.

A Mr. Miller, who lived across the road, took the Lawrences in his car to Mitla. They left Oaxaca at six o'clock in the morning, reaching Mitla after six hours of crawling over what was then a wretched road. An Indian guide directed them among the ruins. They imagined the smell of blood as they stared at the sacrificial stone. Then, somewhat cheered by a hearty lunch at the local restaurant, they took the long drive home.

One afternoon the Lawrences—and Brett, of course— visited a shed where pottery was made. There they watched a clever Indian moulding a bowl as he turned the huge stone wheel with his bare toes. On another occasion Brett, who had a passion for cutlery, went alone to the shop of an Indian whose steel swords and knives were known all over the world. Further entertainment was provided by listening to the town band, and going to see a Douglas Fairbanks picture at the local theatre. Brett bought a baby squirrel in a cage. One evening when Lawrence and Brett, after having cocktails with some friends, got home a little after nine, Frieda became angry. This was the beginning of an unfortunate hostility that was to develop, as it had before, between the two women.

On the day of the Fiesta of San Felipe, Lawrence, Frieda, and Brett entered the Church to find it, in Brett's words, "a sea of kneeling Indians." When they left the Church to wander among the booths, Frieda and Brett ate "large flat cakes with golden syrup," the syrup dripping down their chins. There was a merry-go-round for the children, and the usual beggars squatting in the road.

By this time Lawrence had begun to write *Mornings in Mexico*. He and Brett would walk into the desert, where they would sit, each under a separate bush. There Lawrence would write and Brett would paint, bathed in the radiant sunshine and the fragrant air. When Lawrence had finished writing he would criticize Brett's work, and even try to improve it for her, though he was a writer and she an artist. Soon this collaboration had to stop, however; as Brett tells us, Frieda disapproved of it.

One Sunday morning the Lawrences, accompanied by Rosalino, set out to walk to a certain mountain village, only to find themselves in a different village, that of Huayapa. The men that they met along the road looked askance at Lawrence, while the women looked askance at Frieda. At ten o'clock they paused to rest beside a stream where some cattle were drinking and two native boys were bathing. On entering Huayapa they passed between living fences of organ cactus, with poinsettias and mangos drooping overhead. The village, consisting of black adobe huts surrounded by "chicken-bitten" enclosures, was practically deserted. But there was a white church, a *plaza*, and a fountain. Under a shed, some men were huddled together like conspirators. After a long search the wayfarers succeeded in buying some oranges, limes, and *chirimoyas* for their lunch. These they

93

enjoyed while sitting, relaxed, beside the stream again; and *mañana* seemed a long way off.

On the last Saturday before Christmas Oaxaca enjoyed a very special market day. The air was vibrant with the colors and the scents of bougainvillea, poinsettia, yucca, and hibiscus. White specks of men and women were moving down the slopes of the distant hills, at the beginning of their journey to the town. Their little donkeys, as they approached, were seen to be laden with double baskets—or nets or jars— of merchandise. Many of the women carried babies in the folds of their blue *rebozos*. All these Indians had come to buy and sell, but even more for contact with one another. On one side of the covered market were stalls of fruit and vegetables; on the other, butter, eggs, and cheese. At one end were bright *sarapes* and dark *rebozos*, at the other, *huaraches*, fashioned of woven leather. The sellers shouted and screamed to call attention to their wares. The buyers haggled endlessly. Then, at nightfall, home they went to the hills, men and women and donkeys and all the treasures they had bought. But the only lasting treasure that they carried away with them was the remembrance of human contact.

During the Christmas season Brett, with another woman, attended the Fiesta de los Rábanos. They were somewhat shocked to behold, hanging like dolls in the booths, large pink and white radishes, carved into little lifelike men, with certain portions of their anatomy considerably enlarged. The Indians were amused by their embarrassment. At the same fiesta they joined the natives in buying earthen bowls and throwing them into the air, so that they fell to the ground with a delightful splintering sound. On Christmas day Lawrence was ill in bed, but there was a Christmas

94

tree. Some Indians came with gifts of pottery, and were given presents in return.

In January, 1925, Lawrence wrote to Curtis Brown: "I am sending you four articles—*Mornings in Mexico*—nice and short. . . . I am getting ahead with the Mexican novel. If heaven is with me, I should finish it this month. . . . I like it very much indeed."

Meanwhile the tension between Frieda and Brett had become so strong that something had to snap. Frieda describes the situation thus: "The Brett came every day and I thought she was becoming too much a part of our lives and I resented it. So I told Lawrence: 'I want the Brett to go away,' and he raved at me, said I was a jealous fool. But I insisted and so Brett went up to Mexico City."

According to Brett's version, Rosalino brought to her hotel one morning a letter from Lawrence in which he said that the three of them were no longer "a happy combination" and that they must part. On calling at their house she found Lawrence looking "seedy," and Frieda sitting with her eyes hard and "her mouth a line." The tea table seemed "balanced on a volcano." After Brett had returned to the hotel Lawrence appeared, "excited, stormy, despairing." She offered to leave Oaxaca, and he agreed that this would be for the best. After that Lawrence and Brett enjoyed a few more walks and talks together. Then, one morning, Frieda handed Brett a letter that she had written to her, in which she accused the pair of being "like a curate and a spinster," and *resented* the fact that they did not make love to each other. Although some bitter words were exchanged, Brett and Frieda parted in a friendly way. On the following day the Lawrences put Brett aboard the train for Mexico City.

The letters that Lawrence wrote at this time to Middleton Murry express the most violent antipathy, both towards Murry himself and towards his magazine, the *Adelphi*. He says that he may come back to England in the spring, but that he doesn't expect to see Murry there, because "Last time was once too many."

At last Lawrence finished writing, or revising, his Mexican novel, *Quetzalcoatl*, which was to be renamed *The Plumed Serpent*. In the meantime, however, he had fallen dangerously ill with malaria. In February he wrote to Curtis Brown:

Been having a devil of a time with malaria. . . . That comes of hot winter sun! I hope and pray we can get up to Mexico City in a week's time, out of the malarial areas. With luck we should sail for England from Vera Cruz on March 10th—land in England about March 25th. I shall bring the MS. of *Quetzalcoatl* with me, and you can get it typed for me—then I can go over it. It is finished.

Lawrence's malaria—a serious enough disability in itself—was unfortunately aggravated by a simultaneous attack of the dysentery by which foreigners in the tropics are so frequently stricken. Frieda got a Mexican doctor for him, but the doctor, afraid perhaps to accept so much responsibility, refused the case. The resident English and Americans did everything they could to help. Lawrence swore that he expected to be buried in the local cemetery. "No," laughed Frieda, "it's such an ugly cemetery, don't you think of it."

"But if I die," Lawrence replied, "nothing has mattered but you, nothing at all."

There is a touching humility in Frieda's comment, recorded in *Not I But the Wind*: "I was almost scared to hear him say it, that, with all his genius, I had mattered so much. It seemed incredible."

Frieda comforted Lawrence with hot sand-bags. A missionary's wife, after bringing him a bowl of hot soup, knelt to pray at his bedside. In the middle of the night there was an awful thunder storm, and then an earthquake, which made the roof beams move and which was accompanied by the terrified screams of horses, donkeys, dogs, and cats. On the following day Frieda moved Lawrence over to the hotel, where he could have better care. The journey to Mexico City, a few days later, was "a crucifixion." Frieda had a horrible premonition: "He will never be quite well again, he is ill, he is doomed. All my love, all my strength, will never make him whole again."

Early in March, from the Hotel Imperial in Mexico City, Lawrence wrote to Curtis Brown:

Well, anyhow we've got out of the Valley of Oaxaca. I was so ill down there, with malaria and flu. We are due to sail on the Hamburg-Amerika boat *Rio Bravo* from Vera Cruz on the 17th— land in Plymouth about April 3d. I think we shall stay down in Devonshire for a while, to get strong: doctors say I must be by the sea. Too much altitude in these places.

Then came the crash. The doctor in Mexico City announced that Lawrence had tuberculosis, and that he could live, at the most, only for a year or two. His second letter to Curtis Brown reads:

Still in bed here. Doctor made all sorts of examinations, blood tests, etc. Says I must *not* risk a sea-voyage nor the English climate, for some months; must stay in the sun, either here or go to the ranch. So as soon as I can travel we shall go to the ranch. Write me there.

After a painful tussle with immigration officers on the border, in which the British Consul was forced to intervene, Lawrence and Frieda returned to their ranch in the moun-

97

tains of New Mexico. So ended Lawrence's second and last sojourn in the country below the Rio Grande.

Lawrence described his Oaxaca days in the first four chapters of the slender volume, *Mornings in Mexico,* published in London by Martin Secker in 1927. The remaining four chapters of the volume include three on the Indian dances of New Mexico and Arizona, and one—a brief retrospective fantasy—written much later by the Italian shores of the Mediterranean. All of them display great sensitiveness to beauty, as well as penetrating insight into the hidden meaning of things. They are quite devoid of the ill temper or the tendency towards fine-spun metaphysics found occasionally in other works of Lawrence. They are marred by nothing worse than a number of mistakes in Spanish, for which the author can be forgiven. Though Lawrence was a good linguist, able to speak and write both German and Italian, his Spanish was imperfect. And, like many other English writers of the casual essay, he may have attached less importance to strict accuracy than to charm. For *Mornings in Mexico* is a charming book as well as an instructive one. It is D. H. Lawrence at his best.

TAOS III

LAWRENCE AND FRIEDA were driven from Santa Fe up to Kiowa Ranch by Andrew Dasburg, the painter, and Ida Rauh, the actress. On reaching Kiowa Lawrence told his story to Dorothy Brett, who was there already and who, in *Lawrence and Brett*, recalls his words:

I looked so awful when I reached Mexico City from Oaxaca: just pale green. The people stared at me so in the streets that I could not bear it, so Frieda bought me some rouge. I rouged my cheeks and gave myself such a lovely, healthy complexion that no one even turned to stare at me again. You should have just seen me! I used the rouge all the time until I reached New Mexico—until I got past that terrible doctor at El Paso.

Lawrence was, of course, distressingly thin and pale. For the first few days of April, 1925, he had to spend most of his time lying on the porch, the heavier work being done by the Indian couple, Trinidad and Rufina. It was still cold, but spring was in the air. Brett was living, at Frieda's request, in a cabin on the neighboring ranch of Bill and Rachel Hawk. One morning Bill harnessed Lawrence's two riding horses, Aaron and Ambrose, to a new buggy he had bought. Lawrence insisted on going along. The horses, after a brief rebellion, settled down to a steady trot. But poor Lawrence, as a result of his ride, had to stay in bed for two whole days. On April seventeenth he wrote to Miss Pearn, his typist:

99

I am so thankful to be feeling better, I thought sometimes that I was never going to get out of Mexico, what with malaria, and a typhoid condition inside, and "flu" making my chest go wrong. However, we are on our own ranch, and though I feel still shaky —must lie down most of the time—I am rapidly getting better. It's lovely spring weather up here. . . . We've got an Indian and his wife to do for us: it is good to be quite quiet.

The relations between Frieda Lawrence and Dorothy Brett were, as usual, considerably strained. Brett seemed to feel that Frieda didn't fully appreciate Lawrence, that she didn't take sufficient care of him—that she was, in short, not altogether worthy of him. Frieda, on the other hand, considered Brett as a kind of trespasser on the privacy of her married life. "I did not really want her with us," she writes. "Like the eye of the Lord, she was: when I washed, when I lay under a bush with a book . . . only I hope the eye of the Lord looks on me more kindly." Yet Frieda liked Brett in many ways, freely admitting that she always did her share of the work. She "yelled down her ear-trumpet, her Toby, when people were there, that she should not feel out of it." Brett's visits to the Lawrence cabin were soon restricted, however, to three a week.

Though Mabel Dodge Luhan was living in Taos during the summer of 1925, she and Lawrence did not meet. In fact, they were never to see each other again. Lawrence had failed to write the book that Mabel had brought him to Taos to write, and had written instead a novel set in Mexico. But the following year, when Mabel had finished composing the first volume of *Intimate Memories*, her autobiography, she was to send the manuscript to him in Italy, and he was to continue writing to her as long as he lived.

Lawrence was now working on *David*, the play he had promised to write for Ida Rauh, and Brett was typing it. After it was finished everybody—including Ida herself—

assembled in the Lawrences' living room to hear it read. Frieda lay on her bed smoking. Lawrence, although embarrassed, interpreted the lines of the different characters with the greatest skill. The reading continued, with time out for tea, until evening. Then Lawrence, who was very tired, had to stop. On the following day he began to read again. At the end of the play he looked inquiringly at Ida. To everyone's surprise she said, as Brett relates: "I am too old, Lorenzo; too old to play the part of Michal—so young, so radiant a creature." The others were considerably taken aback.

In the weeks that followed, Lawrence's health improved still more. He was grateful, and the words of Frieda show that she was, too:

How thrilling it was to feel the inrush of new vitality in him; it was like a living miracle. . . . How grateful he was inside him! "I can do things again, I can live and do as I like, no longer held down by the devouring illness." How he loved every minute of life at the ranch! The morning, the squirrels, every flower that came in its turn . . . all assumed the radiance of new life.

As Lawrence's strength returned, he insisted on doing more and more of the work around the ranch. He took part, with several Indians, in digging an irrigation ditch all the way from Gallina Canyon, two miles off. And after Trinidad and Rufina had been dismissed, he split the wood and milked the cow, while Frieda proudly gathered the eight eggs that were laid each day by their eleven hens.

Now is perhaps the appropriate time to touch very briefly on a minor controversy in which Lawrence had become involved with Norman Douglas, the author of *South Wind,* and the widow of Maurice Magnus, that unfortunate individual whom both had known in Italy. Magnus, we recall, had committed suicide in Malta, having borrowed some eighty pounds from "a nice and not rich Maltese" named Michael Borg, whom Lawrence knew and liked. After the death of Magnus it was found that he had left behind him several manuscripts, including an account of his experiences as a member of the French Foreign Legion. In order to help Michael Borg, who was suffering from a nervous breakdown, Lawrence wrote a long introduction to precede Magnus's *Memoirs of the Foreign Legion,* which was then submitted to Martin Secker for publication. Lawrence once told Catherine Carswell, who vouches for his statement, that he considered this introduction "the best single piece of writing, *as writing,* that he had ever done."

Apparently Mrs. Magnus had repudiated her husband before his death, and had subsequently refused to pay his debts. Lawrence felt justified therefore in proposing that royalties from the sale of the *Memoirs* be divided between Michael Borg and himself, Borg to take fifty percent or even more. He asked his agent, Curtis Brown, to settle the legal and commercial details. In due course Curtis Brown sent Lawrence a publication contract, which the latter signed and returned with the stipulation that one-half the royalties were to go to Borg.

Upon the publication of Magnus's *Memoirs of the Foreign Legion,* with Lawrence's introduction, Lawrence was attacked in a pamphlet by Norman Douglas. Douglas claimed to have assisted Magnus in writing his book, and seemed to feel that Lawrence was not entitled to profit by it. He also suggested that Lawrence, in his introduction, had dealt harshly with Magnus. Lawrence, in a letter to Curtis Brown dated April 15, 1925, writes: "Having written half the book, surely half the proceeds are due to me. . . . Besides, Magnus re-wrote the whole thing, after I talked with him in Montecassino. I really sweated to get that fellow money, and

102

Douglas wouldn't give him a cent." And a month later he writes as follows to H. W. Mathews:

Norman Douglas, who is the N. D. of the Florence episode in my introduction, wrote a sort of little pamphlet defending Magnus—and reproaching me. You can get it in London. But Douglas would not question any of the *facts* of the book—he only thinks I am hard on M. M. But in *life* Douglas was much harder on him —very much.

Presently Lawrence received from Douglas a letter which appears to have soothed his feelings somewhat.

Shortly after the departure from Kiowa of Ida Rauh, Frieda's nephew, Friedel Jaffe, came to visit. Friedel, tall, dark, and quite nice looking, was given the tiny cabin formerly occupied by Brett. He was amused, or pretended to be amused, when Lawrence and Frieda quarreled over where to plant some cactus Brett had given them. It was great fun, he thought, to help catch Susan, the refractory cow. He enjoyed a bath at the hot springs with Lawrence and Brett and Bill and Rachel Hawk. This is what Lawrence wrote, towards the end of June, to Catherine Carswell:

We have a black cow, whom I milk every morning and evening, and Frieda collects the eggs—about eight a day—from the eleven hens. Frieda's nephew, Friedel Jaffe, is staying the summer with us—he helps. We had an Indian and his wife to do for us, till last week: then we sent them away. "Savages" are a burden. So a Mexican boy comes up to help, and even him one has to pay two dollars a day. . . . Lovely to think of cherry trees in bloom; here the country is too savage, somehow, for such softness. I get a bit of *Heimweh* for Europe. We shall come in the autumn —D.V.—and winter somewhere warm.

Between Frieda and Brett, all this time, there had prevailed a sort of armed truce. One day, the latter writes, Frieda sent her nephew down to Brett's cabin with a letter suggesting that Brett was "messing up her life." Later the same day, while Lawrence and Brett and Friedel were horseback riding together, Brett declared: "If Frieda starts her . . . nonsense again, I will rope her to a tree and hit her on the nose until she has really something to yell about." Lawrence was too astonished at this to say a word. The subject was changed, presently, to the wonderful days of the Renaissance, and to Lorenzo the Magnificent.

Another storm soon broke between Frieda and Brett. Brett, if we may accept her version of the tale, had accidentally permitted Susan the cow to escape from her corral. Unable to retrieve Susan by herself, she had gone for Lawrence and another man to help her in the search. Lawrence and Brett, when they returned with Susan, found Frieda white with wrath. "I won't have you up here every day," she said to Brett. "You are a mischief-maker. I hate you, hate you!" "Oh, go to hell!" snapped Brett. Frieda retreated in amazement, slamming the door in Brett's face. Yet a few days later Lawrence and Frieda and Brett were enjoying one another's company at tea.

By the end of the summer Lawrence had positively made up his mind to return to Europe; Brett, on the other hand, had formed no definite plans. She wasn't eager to go back to "the old life" in London, and yet to live elsewhere, among strangers, seemed difficult to her because of her deafness. When Lawrence asked her what she was going to do she replied that she would probably remain in New Mexico. Lawrence assured her that her deafness was less of a handicap than she imagined. She was fortunate, he added, to have money, health, and freedom, and she ought to travel. Had she ever been to Italy? No. Well, everybody who could ought to enjoy the beauty of Italy. Brett should go to Capri. He would give her a letter of introduction to the Brewsters there. Brett made no objection, and so it was decided that after the Lawrences had left for England, she would go to Italy.

Lawrence wasn't used to firearms, and didn't like the idea of killing things. However Brett persuaded him, one day, to practice shooting with her 22-calibre rifle. Lawrence selected as his target the doorknob of the outdoor toilet. Shutting the wrong eye, he fired a number of shots which missed the knob but which riddled the door with holes. Then he knelt down, aimed more carefully, and pulled the trigger. The result was a shot that shattered the lock so that the door would never again shut properly. Lawrence was immensely proud of his feat of marksmanship. A few days later he shot a porcupine, an achievement which pleased him and at the same time filled him with remorse. It resulted in the composition of his essay, "Reflections on the Death of a Porcupine."

A journalist named Kyle Crichton wrote to Lawrence asking for an interview. Lawrence, who didn't like to be interviewed, refrained from answering his letters. But Crichton, feeling perhaps that silence gave consent, came up to the ranch anyhow, accompanied by his wife. Fortunately Brett was there to precede them into Lawrence's presence and to "pave the way." When she told him that the Crichtons were "young and tactful and unpushing," he consented to let them in. They proved to be so pleasant that, although he was tired, he spent the entire afternoon with them, drinking tea and providing Crichton with plenty of material for an excellent essay.

Frieda wept when her nephew departed for Germany, but in a little while she was jolly again. She, as well as Lawrence, was permitted to do some work on a large picture that Brett was painting to represent the various activities of the ranch against the background of the desert. Lawrence

declared that every landscape should include some figures.
He and Brett agreed that it was usually best for an artist
to paint from memory. "Why do all the painters have to
sit in front of what they paint?" he queried. "It's because
they feel nothing inside them, so they must have it before
their eyes. . . . It should all be brought from inside oneself."

Lawrence assured Brett that writing was far more difficult
than painting. Brett asked him if he knew, before he started
to write, exactly what it was he was going to say. She has
given us his answer:

No, I never know, when I sit down, just what I am going to
write. I make no plan; it just comes, and I don't know where it
comes from. Of course I have a general sort of outline of what I
want to write about, but when I go out in the mornings I have
no idea what I will write. It just comes, and I really don't know
where from.

Although Lawrence's own writing was so analytical, so
poetical, and so deeply felt, he loved to read the extrover-
ted, machine-made fiction that *Adventure* and other pulp
magazines turned out every month by the yard. He told
Brett it was "simple, unaffected story-telling, sometimes
really very good," and added: "This one I am reading about
the Foreign Legion is very exciting." He didn't seem to
realize that the author of the story had probably never
been any closer to the Foreign Legion than Times Square,
and that his description of it was simply the same conven-
tional picture that had existed in the minds of pulp-writers
and scenario-makers for many a year. Lawrence read with
extreme deliberation, pausing to pronounce each word,
mentally at least, to himself.

Though Lawrence had no children of his own, he was
sometimes deeply affected by the children of others, as is
shown in the following lines addressed to him by Brett:

Suddenly you take Walton [little Walton Hawk] by the shoulders and draw him toward you. You hold him between your knees and look at him intently. Your eyes darken to a deep blue. . . . The child stares back at you solemnly, and puts up a hand to stroke your beard. You release him at last with a sigh.

In September, it was time to close the cabins and prepare to leave. Lawrence and Frieda would go first to England, then to Germany, and finally to Italy, their ultimate destination. "Their eyes are shut," said Lawrence when he saw the cabins with their windows boarded up. "How dismal they look!" He and Frieda stayed overnight with Bill and Rachel Hawk, while Brett remained in her own small cabin, near their house. In the morning she walked behind their car as it started down the mountain on its way towards Taos, gateway to the outer world. Lawrence turned and waved back once before he disappeared. Years later, having left New Mexico never to return, he was to write, in the *Survey Graphic* magazine:

The moment I saw the brilliant, proud morning shine high up over the deserts of Santa Fé something stood still in my soul . . . for a greatness of beauty I have never experienced anything like New Mexico.

And again:

I think New Mexico was the greatest experience from the outside world that I ever had. It certainly changed me forever. Curious as it may sound, it was New Mexico that liberated me from the present era of civilization, the great era of material and mechanical development.

FIRENZE

LAWRENCE AND FRIEDA had returned to England from America on the S. S. *Resolute* at the end of September, 1925. In London Lawrence called on Middleton Murry, in spite of their past differences, bringing with him as a peace offering a bag of fruit. Unfortunately the two became involved in a discussion of religion. Murry defended his rather unusual belief that Judas was the only one of the disciples who really loved Jesus, and that it was the "futility" of the Crucifixion that caused him to hang himself. Lawrence alleged that the personality of Jesus was distasteful to him, and that he couldn't understand why Murry felt obliged to write about Him at all. When they parted they were once more at swords' points.

Before leaving England Lawrence went on a motor trip to his birthplace in the Midlands. He was appalled to see how the natural beauty of Derbyshire had been blighted by industrialism. A blanket of coal-dust lay over everything. Even the churches and the schools were ugly. The workers from the steel mills—twisted, dwarfish men—seemed out of place when they came forth into the light of day. Back in London, Lawrence told Catherine Carswell how, in the course of this trip, "the horrors of his childhood had come up over him like a smothering flood." He hurt her feelings, incidentally, by trying to repay five pounds that she had given Frieda long ago when he was poor.

From London Lawrence went to Baden-Baden to pay his respects to his mother-in-law, whom he had always loved and who was to love him even beyond his own death. In November he and Frieda journeyed to Spotorno, near Genoa on the Italian Riviera di Ponente, where they rented the Villa Bernarda and remained for five months. The villa, which belonged to an Italian army officer, was in charge of an old man named Giovanni, whom they fed. It was probably here that Lawrence wrote his novel *The Virgin and the Gypsy,* which has an English setting rather than a Mexican or an Italian one, and which might have been written before the War. In a letter to his mother-in-law, with whom he always corresponded in German, he describes as follows their new life at Spotorno:

Now it is evening: we are sitting in the kitchen high under the roof. . . . Underneath, the lights of the village lie like oranges and tangerines, little and shining. . . . The soup is boiling. In a moment we call down into the depths: *Vieni, Giovanni, è pronto il mangiare.* Then the old man runs up the stairs like an unhappy frog, with his nose in the air, sniffing and smelling. It is nice for him to know that there is always something good for him to eat.

Presently Frieda sent for her two daughters, Barbara and Else, from whom she had been separated for so many years. Lawrence countered by summoning his sister Ada, who came with her friend Mrs. Booth, and proceeded to antagonize Frieda. Unable to stand the atmosphere of hostility which then developed, Lawrence left for Capri, after accompanying Ada and her friend to Monte Carlo and to Nice.

In Capri Lawrence was met by Dorothy Brett, who had been there for five months, living in the Hotel Internazionale, but watched over by his friends the Brewsters. The latter put him up at their villa, Quattro Venti. He looked so pale and tired that Brett could scarcely bear the sight of him. Of their first walk together she writes:

How lovely a day it is! The sea is so clear that I can see the shells and stones and glistening sea-weed at the bottom. And what a blue! You and I are sitting on the sands of the Piccola Marina. The walk down the narrow, stony path, down the endless, uneven stone steps, tires you a little; but lying full-length on the hot sand, relaxed, brings your strength back again.

They called on Branford, an ailing poet with a beauteous wife and a little girl who thought that the bearded Lawrence was "Father Christmas." They called also on Mrs. Compton Mackenzie, who told them that her novelist husband was away on one of the Channel Islands. Lawrence reverted constantly to his longing to own a yacht, manned by a captain and a couple of sailors, so that he might turn his back on trouble and go sailing off to the Isles of Greece. In the evening, at the Quattro Venti, while the winds raged outside, he drank wine and sang old English ballads with Brett and the Brewsters, until his cares were, momentarily at least, forgotten. He also led the others in charades, which had always been one of his favorite pastimes. And he told the story of "The Rocking Horse Winner," urging the other guests to contribute additional stories to a volume to be called, after the name of the villa, *Tales of the Four Winds*. With the proceeds from the volume they could buy their yacht. Lawrence and Brett climbed up to the Rock of Tiberius, from which the Roman Emperor's unfortunate enemies had been tossed down into the sea. As they sat there Lawrence fell asleep. Brett writes:

I sit and watch you. The sun pours down relentlessly on your head; a heavy lock of hair falls over your face; your beard glitters red in the sun. As I watch you, the meaningless modern suit seems to drop away. A leopard skin, a mass of flowers and leaves wrap themselves round you. Out of your thick hair, two small horns poke their sharp points; the slender, cloven hoofs lie entangled in weeds. The flute slips from your hand. I stare at you in a kind of trance.

Later, at her hotel. Brett showed Lawrence her painting of Christ on the Cross. Near the foot of the Cross sat Pan, tempting the Master with a bunch of grapes. The deep blue Mediterranean lay in the background of the picture, while in the foreground could be seen the top of the tower of the Villa dei Quattro Venti. Christ's head and Pan's head both resembled the head of Lawrence.

Brett accompanied Lawrence on a sea voyage to Amalfi and to Ravello, where he wanted to see his painter friends, Miss Beveridge and Miss Harrison. In Ravello they stopped at the Hotel Palumbo, which had been the Bishop's Palace and which is now the residence of the Duca di Sangro. There Lawrence ate a huge beefsteak, to recover from the Brewsters' vegetarianism. He and Brett wandered over to the Villa Cimbrone, built by Lord Grimthorpe and later occupied, so it is said, by Stokowski and Greta Garbo. In its gardens they discovered a statue—a blue Venus—of which each made a painting. "My eye catches sight of a white violet," Brett writes. "I pick it and hand it to you. You hold it with that strange tenderness that flowers bring to your hands. . . . There is radiance everywhere. The white violet shines." Back at Amalfi Brett took the boat for Naples, where she made arrangements for her return to America, to New Mexico, and to the Del Monte Ranch. She would never see Lawrence again.

Lawrence had sent to Frieda a drawing of Jonah and the whale, with the caption: "Who is going to swallow whom?" Frieda's daughters were so amused by this that they implored their mother to make peace with him. Since she had married him, they argued, she must accept him as he was. So when Lawrence returned to Spotorno, after pausing deliberately at Rome, Perugia, Assisi, and Florence, he found all three of them at the railroad station, ready to welcome him in their Sunday best.

In April, 1926, the Lawrences left Spotorno and went to Florence. After Barbara and Else had returned to England they took the Villa Mirenda at Scandicci, about seven miles from Florence in the pine-clad hills. It had been recommended to them by their friend Orioli, English-speaking proprietor of a Florentine bookstore. Frieda describes their discovery of the villa thus:

It was April, the young beans were green and the wheat and peas up, and we drove into the old Tuscan landscape, that perfect harmony of what nature did and man made. . . . Beyond Scandicci we passed two cypresses and went to the left on a small, little used road. On the top of one of those Tuscan hills stood a villa. My heart went out to it. . . . It was . . . so perfectly placed, with a panorama of the Valdarno in front, Florence on the left, and the umbrella-pine woods behind.

The ground floor of the Mirenda was used by the owner as a wine cellar. The rooms on the second story formed the four sides of a square. At the very top of the villa was a glass-enclosed belvedere, from which a magnificent view of Florence and of the Valdarno could be had. The Villa Mirenda was to be the Lawrences' home, with occasional absences, for the next three years. Of their sojourn there Richard Aldington, in his introduction to *Apocalypse*, has written: "Lawrence's return to Tuscany was fortunate. I think he always liked it, and was as happy at the Mirenda as anywhere, except perhaps the Ranch and Sicily."

It was fun to shop in Florence, with their servants Pietro

and Giulia, for the simple things they needed to furnish the Mirenda. Lawrence made a kitchen table and put up brackets for the pots and pans. They painted the shutters and the chairs, and put grass mats on the red tile floors. The walls were freshly sprayed with white. Later they would be decorated with pictures painted by Lawrence himself.

In the afternoon the Lawrences went for walks in the country. They heard the peasants singing at their work, and the creaking of the wheel as they drew water from a well. There were carpets of violets in the woods, and tufts of primroses in the valley. There were anemones, tulips, orchids, and lavender, "like the ground," thought Frieda, "in a Fra Angelico picture." In the fields they saw white oxen ploughing between the cypresses.

Early in June the cicadas were shrilling in the trees, and the girls in the fields were singing as they cut the corn. The sheaves of wheat lay "like people dead asleep in the heat." Lawrence was writing nothing but an occasional article. As he wrote his London publisher, Martin Secker: "Why do any more books? There are so many, and such a small demand for what there are." Towards the end of June he wrote to Dorothy Brett, in New Mexico:

I am very much better in health, now I can go about in shirt and trousers and sandals, and it's hot, and all relaxed. We live very quietly, picnic by the stream sometimes. I have finished typing and revising *David* in German— he was a job! Did I tell you I had the little typewriter taken apart and cleaned? It goes very nicely. But I'm glad it's shut up again, it is an irritable thing, a typewriter.

To Mabel Dodge Luhan he wrote:

Am glad you like Taos: it *is* very lovely there, with the fine pure air. I continue to like Tuscany: the cicadas are rattling away in the sun, the bells of all the little churches are ringing midday,

113

the big white oxen are walking slowly home from under the olives. There is something eternal about it.

In mid-July the Lawrences left Italy to spend a couple of months in Germany and England. In London Lawrence renewed his acquaintance with Aldous Huxley, who had met him for the first time in 1915. They were drawn to each other, both as friends and as master and disciple, and the brilliant young novelist was thenceforth to spend much time with Lawrence—in Italy, Switzerland, and France—until the latter's death. In his best-known novel, *Point Counter Point*, Mark and Mary Rampion suggest D. H. and Frieda Lawrence.

In August, after a trip to Scotland, which he found too cold and rainy, Lawrence was back again in London. He and Frieda returned to Florence on October fourth, just in time to see—and smell—the harvesting of the grapes. On the warm afternoons Lawrence would sometimes sit in a deck chair behind the villa with a friend. Presently a shy Italian child would come stealing through the shrubbery with a bunch of grapes in his grubby hand. Lawrence, feigning surprise, would ask: "What have you got there?"

And the child would answer: "Grapes, Signor Lorenzo." "For me?"

"Sissignore." Then Lawrence, no matter how tired he might be, would get up and enter the house to fetch a piece of chocolate for the grubby child, for he knew how terribly poor the Italian peasants were, and how desperately their children needed nourishment.

Richard Aldington came to visit at the Villa Mirenda. In December Aldous and Maria Huxley drove up in a nice new car, to spend the day. Aldous thought that Lawrence too should have a car, but Lawrence wasn't interested. He didn't care to "struggle with a machine," or

114

to "scud about the face of the country." It was pleasanter, he thought, just to "go quietly into the pine woods and sit" and do what bit of work he did. On four unused canvases, which Maria Huxley had left behind her, he painted the first of his rather daring pictures. He mixed his paints on a piece of glass, and painted not only with brushes but also with his fingers and the palm of his hand. Now and then he would call on Frieda to provide him with the model for an arm or a leg.

The day before Christmas, at four o'clock in the morning, the Lawrences' servant Pietro arrived at the Mirenda with a Christmas tree he had cut for them in the woods. Lawrence and Frieda, aided by Pietro and Giulia, trimmed the tree with gold and silver cones, silver threads, and candies. Then it was hung with toys for the peasant children, many of whom had never had toys before. Twenty-seven of the country folk, on Christmas Day, were invited to the celebration. While the children handled their wooden toys with awe, their fathers reveled in cigars and wine.

At the close of December Lawrence wrote to Maria Huxley: "I like it here. I told you we'd fixed up the *salotto* nice and warm, with matting and stove going and Vallombroso chairs. If you find a villa, find one between here and Galuzzo, if you can, so I can walk over." A few weeks later he wrote to Dorothy Brett: "I've nearly done my novel— shall let it lie and settle down a bit before thinking of having it typed." The novel referred to is *Lady Chatterley's Lover*, a sincere piece of writing which was to be read by the wrong people and for the wrong reasons, and to involve Lawrence in many difficulties.

In March, 1927, while Frieda was in Germany, Lawrence went to visit his friends the Brewsters, who were staying at Ravello. In a talkative mood he told young Harwood, who called him "Uncle David," stories of his boyhood. He expressed his preference for new pictures instead of old. He served as a model for Achsah while she painted, but wouldn't keep still, insisting that life is motion, and that you must capture it if you can. He sang folksongs in English, German, and French. With regard to his own work, he predicted it would be three hundred years before he would be understood. "Each human relationship," he said, "should be a glorious rainbow." Excessively sensitive as he was, the profanity—or obscenity— of a couple of Italian coachmen could ruin a whole afternoon for him.

Lawrence and Brewster, in the gardens of the Villa Cimbrone, revisited the Blue Venus. They also discovered a modern Eve which Lawrence disliked so much that he covered it with mud. The two friends went together to Sorrento. Then they set forth on a tour of the ancient Etruscan towns. On Easter morning at Grosseto, Earl, seeing in a shop window a toy white rooster escaping from an egg, gave Lawrence the title for his story of the Resurrection, "The Escaped Cock." Later Earl deplored the title, while declaring that the story is perhaps "the most beautiful writing Lawrence has left us." The first part of it was published under its original title in an American magazine, *The Forum,* while the complete version appeared in England as a book, *The Man Who Died.*

People would be more interested in the Etruscans, Lawrence thought, if they had not been dazzled by the Greeks, and if they had not been misled by the remarks of Roman writers, to the effect that the Etruscans were "vicious" or "immoral." Ancient Etruria consisted of twelve cities, having much in common from a cultural point of view while preserving a considerable amount of political independence. Since the Etruscan cities were built of wood they have completely disappeared, except for their fortifying walls and their tombs, which lay outside the city limits. Lawrence, pleased with this transitory type of construction, says of it in *Etruscan Places*:

I like to think of the little wooden temples of the early Greeks and of the Etruscans: small, dainty, fragile, and evanescent as flowers. We have reached the stage when we are weary of huge stone erections, and we begin to realize that it is better to keep life fluid and changing than to try to hold it fast down in heavy monuments. Burdens on the face of the earth are man's ponderous erections.

At Cerveteri Lawrence and Brewster found Etruscan tombs occupying a collection of mounds. Inside the mounds were stone houses with ledges which supported stone sarcophagi. Here the illustrious dead were laid to rest, while the ashes of their slaves reposed nearby in urns. The heavy tombs were designed with a simplicity which had "the natural beauty of the phallic consciousness." The tomb of the Tarquins had inscriptions on the walls, as well as carvings of animals and of ornamental objects. Death, to the Etruscans, was neither a descent into the flames of hell nor a soaring aloft to heavenly bliss; it was a continuance, on an earthly plane, of the pleasant things of life.

The chief city of the Etruscans was Tarquinia, near Cività Vecchia on the shore of the Mediterranean. On their way to the site of this ancient city the two companions passed through a region which induced Lawrence to remark that today "the flowers of the coastline are miserable bathing-places such as Ladispoli and seaside Ostia, desecration put upon desolation, to the triumphant trump of the mosquito!" However the countryside around Tarquinia was beautiful, and in the town they discovered a handsome palace which had been transformed into a museum. In this

museum, the Palazzo Vitelleschi, there were innumerable
Etruscan vases and stone sarcophagi surmounted with
carven effigies. A guide took Lawrence and his friends to
the necropolis on a hill outside the city walls. Climbing
down into one underground cell after another, they found
that the walls of the tombs were painted with all sorts of
bright and lively scenes. Each tomb had been named in
accordance with the pictures on its walls, and was called
the Tomb of Hunting and Fishing, the Tomb of the Leop-
ards, the Tomb of the Bacchanti, the Tomb of the Maiden,
the Tomb of the Old Man, or the Tomb of the Bulls. There
were twenty-five such tombs, dating back as far as the sixth
century B.C. On one of the walls of nearly every tomb there
was painted a banquet scene, with men and women eating
and drinking together at a well-served table. The man who
had died was depicted holding up an egg, which Lawrence
calls the Egg of the Resurrection, for all the guests to see.

Vulci and Volterra, the other two Etruscan towns that
Lawrence and Brewster visited, proved less rewarding than
the others. Vulci, to which they were taken in a carriage,
lay near the Maremma, a malaria-ridden coastal plain. The
site of the town, which had disappeared, was marked by
nothing more than a tower and a bridge. In the excavation
of the tombs, which had been begun by Lucien Bonaparte,
brother of Napoleon, the black Etruscan pottery had been
destroyed, and treasures of all kinds had gone to join collec-
tions in Rome, in Florence, or in London. Nothing remained
but stone coffins, bones, and rubble. Bats were everywhere.

On a towering bluff thirty miles from the Mediterranean
stood Volterra. In the modern town the two friends watched
some artisans who were carving the soft Volterra marble
into lamp-bowls and other ornaments for exportation to
various parts of the world. The local museum was filled with

alabaster chests for storing the ashes of the dead. Some of these were carved with sea monsters, griffins, and other mythological beasts, while some displayed banquet scenes, hunting scenes, or scenes of battle. The chests, about two feet long, had lids on which reclined a figure of the man or woman who had died. The few tombs that could still be found in the vicinity of the town seemed unimportant.

Lawrence had a theory that the Etruscans degenerated sadly after the Roman conquest in the third century B.C. It was these degenerate Etruscans, described by classical writers, with whom modern scholars were familiar. Yet in present-day Italy, he thought, one could find "faces still jovial with Etruscan vitality, beautiful with the mystery of the unrifled ark, ripe with the phallic knowledge and the Etruscan carelessness." This observation led him to make the following statement, which is certainly a powerful summing-up of the Lawrentian philosophy:

Brute force crushes many plants. Yet the plants rise again. The Pyramids will not last a moment compared with the daisy. And before Buddha or Jesus spoke, the nightingale sang, and long after the words of Jesus and Buddha are gone into oblivion the nightingale still will sing. Because it is neither preaching nor teaching nor commanding nor urging. It is just singing. And in the beginning was not the Word, but a chirrup.

The excursion that Lawrence made with Brewster as his companion was to result in the publication, in 1932, of *Etruscan Places,* a series of essays in which the author reveals exceptional insight as an archeologist. In this volume there are comparatively few pages of the tenuous mysticism in which he occasionally indulged. Nor does it contain an excessive amount of railing against unsatisfactory inns, bad meals, and annoying "natives." Lawrence gives us a graphic description of the Etruscan tombs, and speculates with

119

extraordinary clairvoyance on the lives of the men and women who were finally laid to rest within their painted walls. He comments thus on the Etruscans, in his poem "Cypresses," from *Birds, Beasts and Flowers*:

> Were they then vicious, the slender, tender-footed
> Long-nosed men of Etruria?
> Or was their way only evasive and different, dark,
>   like cypress-trees in a wind?
> They are dead, with all their vices,
> And all that is left
> Is the shadowy monomania of some cypresses
> And tombs.

In April, when Lawrence and Brewster had finished their Etruscan tour, the former rejoined his wife at the Villa Mirenda, the latter his wife and daughter in southern Italy. Back again in Scandicci, Lawrence proceeded with the writing of *Lady Chatterley's Lover*. Concerning its creation Frieda Lawrence recalls:

After breakfast . . . he would take his book and pen and a cushion, followed by John the dog, and go into the woods behind the Mirenda and come back to lunch with what he had written. I read it day by day and wondered how his chapters were built up and how it all came to him. I wondered at his courage and daring to face and write these hidden things that people dare not write or say. . . . For two years *Lady Chatterley* lay in an old chest that Lawrence had painted a greeny yellow with roses on it, and often when I passed that chest I thought: "Will that book ever come out of there?"

Many references to the new novel are to be found in Lawrence's letters at the time. He had written to Miss Pearn on the twenty-second of March: "I must go over it again and am really not sure if I shall publish it—at least this year. And I think it is *utterly* unfit for serializing—they would call it indecent— though really it's most decent." On April

12th he wrote to Miss Pearn again: "It's what the world would call very improper. But . . . I always labor at the same thing, to make the sex-relation valid and precious, instead of shameful." And on April 29th he wrote to his publisher, Martin Secker: "I've been thinking about *Lady Chatterley's Lover* and think I'll get him typed in London before long, and let you have a copy, so you can see how possible or impossible he is. But there is much more latitude these days, and a man dare possibly possess a penis."

The spring of 1927 was as beautiful in Florence as it had been the previous year. But Lawrence caught a cold, which resulted in a bronchial hemorrhage. During his convalescence he sometimes had to pause for breath while walking in the fields. Because of his diminished strength—and perhaps for other reasons too—he declined an urgent invitation, received in April from Mabel Dodge Luhan, to return to Taos. Even by the end of May he still felt unable to go to London for the opening of his play *David*. *David* was less successful, it turned out, than his other play, *The Widowing of Mrs. Holroyd,* had been a few months previously. In June a hundred-mile excursion to the sea at Forte dei Marmi, where Lawrence went bathing with the Huxleys, brought on congestion of the lungs. Feeling better after his return to Florence, he wrote to Else, his German sister-in-law (for whom one of Frieda's daughters had been named):

It is very hot here, too hot to sit in the sun for breakfast, even before seven in the morning. One gets up early, then has a siesta in the afternoon. Frieda is still peacefully slumbering . . . and not a soul is alive on all the *poderi*—peasants sleeping too. The Arno valley lies hot and still in the sun, but there is a little breeze, so I shall go down and sit on the grass in a deck chair under the nespole tree.

121

Later in June Earl Brewster visited the Lawrences at the Villa Mirenda to tell them of his recent travels in India and Greece. Brewster admired the pictures Lawrence had painted and hung on the walls. They walked together over the Tuscan hills. A neighbor's dog, who always joined them on their walks, would steal eggs from the farms along the way, but would always bring them to Lawrence and ask his permission before eating them. Writing to the Huxleys in July, Lawrence first complained of his bad health and then went on: "We'll send the books back. Proust too much water-jelly—I can't read him. *Faux-monnayeurs* was interesting as a revelation of the modern state of mind, but it's done to shock and surprise . . . not real."

In August Lawrence went with Frieda to Austria, where his condition improved. From there, in September, they journeyed to the German Isarthal, and stayed for a month in the same little Bavarian chalet where, fifteen years before, they had spent their honeymoon. Here Lawrence translated Verga's tale "Cavalleria Rusticana," and wrote the introduction for his collection of that author's stories. A little later he took some inhalations at Baden-Baden. Thence, on October twentieth, they returned to their home in Florence.

At the Villa Mirenda, in November, Lawrence rewrote *Lady Chatterley's Lover* for the second time. He also painted more of his somewhat startling pictures, including one of Adam and Eve chasing God the Father out of Eden. The Carswells attempted to persuade him to spend Christmas with them in the Harz Mountains, where a German lung specialist had offered to treat him for a small fee or none at all. But he preferred to pass Christmas Eve with the peasants at the Villa Mirenda, and Christmas Day with the Huxleys in Florence. Aldous Huxley had benefited much by Lawrence's creed, and Lawrence had in him a friend on whom he could rely. It was with him and his wife and the Julian Huxleys that Lawrence and Frieda went, in January, 1928, to the Swiss resort of Les Diablerets, whose four-thousand-foot altitude had been recommended. Though Lawrence couldn't participate in any of the winter sports, his health was benefited. In February, while Frieda was in Baden-Baden, the Huxleys cared for him solicitously.

Lady Chatterley's Lover, which was first called *Tenderness* and later *John Thomas and Lady Jane,* had been rejected by two London publishers. Lawrence, on returning to the Villa Mirenda in March, determined to publish the novel privately, in a limited edition of one thousand copies. He and the bookseller Orioli found a Florentine print shop whose proprietor, Franceschini, knew no English, and which had only type enough to print one-half the book at a time, but which would do the job for a sum he thought he could afford. The proofs, with their innumerable errors, kept Lawrence busy during April and May. He sent announcements of *Lady Chatterley* to all his friends, urging them to publicize it as widely as possible. "We shall never sell all these!" cried Frieda, when she saw the stacks and stacks of *Our Lady,* as they dubbed the book, piled high on the printer's floor, each copy stamped on its red cover with Lawrence's emblem, a black phoenix rising from its nest in flames. But the books, though printed on hand-made cream-colored paper and priced at a couple of pounds, sold fast. Lawrence's "last great effort," his "phallic novel," as he called it—was a success, even though he was abused in England, and even though a dozen pirated editions appeared in the United States and elsewhere, from which he never received a penny.

The plot and nature of *Lady Chatterley's Lover* are too well known to need discussion here. Individual readers have long since formed their various opinions of Mellors, the virile game-keeper who slept with the wife of his employer, a man whose health had been injured in World War I. They have long since been either amused or disgusted or simply bored by all the four-letter words which, in 1928, provided a novel experience for readers of fiction. Frieda said that Lawrence, in writing *Lady Chatterley's Lover*, was speaking of and for his own class, which was sure to profit from it. According to Hugh Kingsmill, the novel is "an attempt to obliterate his social and his sexual mortification." Middleton Murry calls it "an utterly hopeless book . . . with its simple and monotonous insistence that physical fulfilment between man and woman is the be-all and end-all of human existence." But Murry explains this insistence on the basis of the author's own sexual shortcomings, for which, if they existed, poor Lawrence certainly was not to blame. Rebecca West has expressed most beautifully the viewpoint of those who credit Lawrence with having attempted, in *Lady Chatterley's Lover* to do something truly fine:

His claim to our reverence and gratitude was not in the least part diminished by *Lady Chatterley's Lover*. It is an appalling fact that man should speak of the functions on which depend the continued existence of his species and the tender life of the heart in words that cause shame and ugly laughter when they are spoken. When Lawrence's pity was aroused by this wound in the side of life he did what saints do: he asked for a miracle. He laid sex and those base words for it on the salver of his art and held them up before the consciousness of the world, which was his way of approaching creation, and prayed that both might be transmuted to the highest that man could use.

After the publication of *Lady Chatterley's Lover* Lawrence's health disintegrated rapidly. When he had another hemorrhage it was all that Frieda and Dr. Giglioli and Giulia could do to nurse him back to health. In a letter

124

written at this time to Frieda's sister Else he reveals a flash of insight into the true source of all his physical suffering:

My illnesses I know come from chagrin—that goes deep in and comes out afterwards in hemorrhage or what not. When one learns . . . not to be chagrined, then one can become like your Bürgomeister . . . fat and *lustig*, to the age of eighty . . . I'd be glad to be fat and *lustig* once before I die—even a bit *versoffen*, if that's a way of not having a sore chest.

Because Lawrence had been desperately ill in Florence, he now wanted to leave that city. When he started to pack his paintings, though, Frieda became so sad that he leased the Villa Mirenda for six months more. After a month or two, anxious to go to Switzerland, he offered it to Earl and Achsah Brewster. But the Brewsters, like the loyal friends they were, decided instead to go with him and Frieda to the Alps. This they did, traveling by train to Torino, Chambéry, Aix-les-Bains, Grenoble, while Lawrence, in fine fettle, led the group in singing hymns.

CONCLUSION

NEAR GRENOBLE, at Saint-Nizier-de-Pariset, the Lawrences and the Brewsters discovered a charming inn; but Lawrence, because of his cough, was not permitted to remain. Moving on to Vevey, they established themselves there for several weeks. Frieda left the group to visit her mother in Baden-Baden. Lawrence waited anxiously for her return. On the day of her arrival he met train after train without success, only to find that she had returned to Vevey by motor.

In July the Lawrences took a chalet high up in the mountains at Gsteig-bei-Gstaadt, with the Brewsters in a hotel some distance below. Here Lawrence, using as his desk a rustic bench in the pine-wood, wrote newspaper articles— something he had never done before—while Earl Brewster amused himself by painting mountain scenes. Lawrence criticized his friend's work freely, as he always did, meanwhile doing some water colors of his own. He also read aloud a fragment of his unfinished novel, *The Flying Fish*, which was based on his narrow escape from death in Oaxaca. By the end of August he had completed the second part of his tale, *The Man Who Died*, the first part of which had been published in *The Forum* eighteen months previously. Since the Brewsters were leaving for Geneva, he

126

decided to offer them a farewell party. On this hilarious occasion he baptized their Hindu friend, Boshi Sen, with wine. Boshi sang a Sanskrit hymn. Lawrence chanted Mexican love songs, ending in a war-whoop. All this in the presence of his decorous sister, whom he called "Pamela, or Virtue Rewarded."

The two couples were together again in Baden-Baden in September and October of 1928. They all stayed at the Hotel Löwen, which had a charming garden. A famous physician there offered to examine Lawrence, but the latter declined. He spent hours playing patience with his mother-in-law, and listening to the singing of a workman's choral society. The Brewsters and the Lawrences drank the medicinal waters and enjoyed the concerts of the orchestra that played in the Kursaal. They celebrated Earl's fiftieth birthday with a magnificent drive through the Black Forest. On October second Frieda went to Florence to close the Villa Mirenda, where she and her husband had lived so long and where, in spite of everything, they had tasted so much happiness. The Villa, the surrounding pine-woods, and the peasants, Frieda thought, "seemed sad at being left." After Frieda's departure from Baden-Baden, Lawrence and the Brewsters journeyed together to Strasbourg. From there the Brewsters returned to Capri, while Lawrence went to join the Huxleys and Frieda's daughter Else at Le Lavandou, east of Toulon on the French Riviera.

When Frieda arrived at Le Lavandou, accompanied by Richard Aldington and Brigit Patmore, all accepted Aldington's invitation to stay at "La Vigie," on the Ile de Port-Cros. From "La Vigie," at night, they could see the twinkling lights of Toulon, Le Lavandou, and Hyères. Frieda and Brigit did the cooking. Lawrence wrote a little and painted a little. He read *Point Counter Point* with enjoyment. Exasperated, however, by Aldous Huxley's depiction of him as Mark Rampion, he expressed his pique in the following lines, which Hugh Kingsmill quotes:

> I read a novel by a friend of mine
> in which one of his characters was me,
> the novel it sure was mighty fine
> but the funniest thing that could be
>
> was me, or what was supposed to be me. . . .
>
> well damn my eyes! I said to myself,
> well damn my little eyes!
> if this is what Archibald thinks I am
> he sure thinks a lot of lies.

He suffered from the attacks, in *John Bull* and in *The Sunday Chronicle*, on *Lady Chatterley's Lover*. And a spell of influenza forced him to remain inside the house.

Forsaking Port-Cros on November fourteenth, Lawrence and Frieda settled tentatively at Bandol, on the French Riviera between Toulon and Marseilles. Here Katherine Mansfield too had stayed, when she was desperately ill. Lawrence, enjoying the scenery and climate at Bandol, felt somewhat better. He and Frieda sipped their daily *apéritifs* at a colorful cafe on the waterfront. In the meantime he was composing the short poems called *Pansies*. During the winter that he spent at Bandol, a representative of the Mandrake Press called to propose a volume of reproductions of his paintings, to be published at the time of his London exhibition, now scheduled for the following summer. After some hesitation, Lawrence agreed to write an introduction for the volume. It would sell at a very substantial price, and he hoped to make considerable money out of it. In January he finished the introduction and sent

128

it to his London agent, Curtis Brown. Here it was seized, and temporarily impounded, by the police, together with the manuscript of *Pansies*.

In March, 1929, Lawrence went to Paris to attend to various business, including the publication of an inexpensive edition of *Lady Chatterley's Lover*, which would compete against the pirated editions then being sold in London and New York. While stopping at the Hotel de Versailles, in the Boulevard Montparnasse, he wrote a preface for this edition. In spite of the illness resulting from his exertion, he then decided to take Frieda, who had arrived from Bandol by way of Baden-Baden on March twenty-seventh, on a long and arduous journey to Mallorca.

The Lawrences stopped to rest at Toulouse and at Barcelona. The latter city was teeming with life, but impressed Lawrence as being essentially proletarian. On reaching Palma de Mallorca they went to stay at the Hotel Principe Alfonso. In the beginning Lawrence experienced a period of lassitude and dejection. The people depressed him, and he had a touch of something to which he referred as "malaria." But presently he revived sufficiently to become quite enthusiastic over the mountains and the sea. He and Frieda were driven to the monastery at Valdemosa, whose cloisters had witnessed the loves of Chopin and George Sand. They picnicked on a bluff above the Mediterranean, to the shores of which they had clung for so many years of their lives. In some walled garden they believed they felt the presence of the Moors. But Lawrence couldn't seem to buckle down to work in Mallorca. Accordingly, on June eighteenth, they departed for Marseilles. From there Lawrence returned to Italy and visited his friends the Huxleys at the seaside resort of Forte dei Marmi. Frieda, in the meantime, went to London to attend the exhibition of his paintings, which had opened on June fourteenth at Dorothy Warren's gallery.

Simultaneously with the opening of the exhibition, the Mandrake Press brought out the volume of colored prints for which Lawrence had written an introduction. Both the exhibition and the book succeeded far beyond his fondest hopes. Twelve thousand people visited the gallery. But Lawrence's enemies were, unfortunately, on the alert. Pretending that some of his paintings were "indecent," they instigated legal proceedings in the course of which the pictures were actually threatened with destruction, and which resulted in the closing of the show. This ugly incident undoubtedly undermined still further Lawrence's health, and may indeed have even shortened his life.

At Forte dei Marmi, Lawrence became seriously ill. Maria Huxley drove him to Florence, where he was obliged to spend a couple of days in bed in his friend Orioli's apartment. He was dejected by the news that his paintings had been confiscated. But the arrival of Frieda, to whom Orioli had sent a telegram, cheered him up. As soon as Lawrence was able to leave Italy, he and Frieda set out for Germany again. At Baden-Baden there was a party to celebrate Frieda's fiftieth birthday. Perhaps because the people around them seemed so healthy, Lawrence felt depressed. It was then that he began to write his beautiful poems on death.

At about this time Lawrence's paintings were returned to him by the police, on condition that he would not exhibit them again. Four copies of the *Album* had been burned. Lawrence, in his letters, cried out against England. He declared that he would never return to his native country; and, as a matter of fact, he never did. He planned to establish, with Rhys Davies and Charles Lahr, a "little magazine" called *Satire,* in which he would attack his enemies. He

130

actually wrote twenty-five satirical poems to which he gave the title *Nettles*. On August twenty-fifth he and Frieda left Baden-Baden for Bavaria. They spent three weeks at Rottach, on the Tegernsee, where Dr. Max Mohr, a physician and writer, had found a cabin for them. Here Lawrence experimented briefly with a vegetarian diet. On September eleventh he celebrated his forty-fourth birthday. On the 17th he and Frieda and Max Mohr left for the French Riviera.

Once more the Lawrences settled at Bandol. Once more they engaged rooms at the Hotel Beau Rivage, while Mohr stayed at another hotel near by. On the first of October they took the Villa Beau Soleil, which some opulent lover, in bygone years, had evidently had constructed for the lady of his heart, and which was not only adorned with cupids but also provided with every sort of *confort moderne,* including central heating, which Lawrence, who preferred an open fire, despised. However he delighted in the view, from his bedroom window, of the sea and of the islands off the coast. He now began to write the book that was to be his last—*Apocalypse,* a commentary on the Book of Revelation. By day and by night he kept his curtains raised and his windows wide, as if to remain in touch as long as possible with the sea, the sun, the moon, and the stars.

Once the Lawrences were comfortably established at the Villa Beau Soleil, Max Mohr went home to Germany. Earl and Achsah Brewster, arriving towards the end of October, rented a farmhouse not too far away but decidedly primitive in its appointments. Because it had open fires Lawrence preferred it to the Beau Soleil. In mid-December Ida Rauh, the actress, came to Bandol. Harwood Brewster, arriving to spend her Christmas holidays from school, typed *Apocalypse* for Lawrence. The latter was quite pleased when

131

Harwood, whose teacher had asked her to write an essay on some great man, chose as her subject "My Uncle David." After Christmas Lawrence's sister Ada made a visit, as did Frieda's sister Else. Barbara, Frieda's daughter, established herself more or less permanently as Lawrence's secretary. At about this time Lawrence wrote to Mabel Dodge Luhan that in the spring he and Frieda would return to Taos, where he still desired to establish a colony of young people for whom he would be a sort of teacher.

Earl Brewster tried to relieve poor Lawrence's discomfort by massaging him with cocoanut oil. Lawrence told him: "I intend to find God: I wish to realize my relation with him." At this time he was writing more of his splendid death poems. He was also reading Moffatt's translation of the *Bible*, Dean Inge on Plotinus, and Gilbert Murray on the Greek religion. This is not surprising, for, as T. S. Eliot has remarked, Lawrence, "without being a Christian, was primarily and always religious." On the advice of Dr. Morland, a physician sent to him by friends in England, he took a good deal of rest. Someone had given him a yellow kitten, Mickie Mussolini, and two goldfish in a bowl. Lawrence scolded Mickie severely when, one day, she caught both fish and ate them. Meanwhile his health was getting worse. All visitors, even the Brewsters, were now forbidden to him. The letters that he wrote to Mabel and Brett, toward the end of January, were the last they would ever receive from him.

On the first of February, 1930, Frieda and Earl took Lawrence, by way of Toulon and Antibes, up to the hill-town of Vence, where he was given a room in the sanatorium Ad Astra. The room had walls of what he described as "overpowering blue," but it overlooked the mountains and the Mediterranean which he loved so much. He was fairly

contented for a time. H. G. Wells came to visit him, and
the Aga Khan, and the Huxleys. Jo Davidson made a sculp-
ture of his head. The library of the sanatorium seemed to
contain little more than French translations of Walter Scott.
However he discovered and began to read a life of Columbus. Did he feel that he too, in a little while, would be
setting forth on a voyage of discovery towards another
world?

After a couple of weeks poor Lawrence's condition grew
even worse. He suffered a good deal of pain. Half admitting
that he might be going to die, he asked, in that event, to
be buried simply. Barbara came up from Bandol to help
her mother care for him. Frieda sat all through the nights
on a cane chair in his room. She thought, in her solitude, of
her first meeting with him, of their first days together.
Sometimes her revery would be interrupted by the cries of
pain and sorrow that came from the adjoining rooms.

After a month at the sanatorium Lawrence, though he
was terribly ill, expressed a desire to leave. On the first of
March (St. David's Day!) Frieda took him in a taxi to the
Villa Robermond. As he lay in bed she continued reading to
him from the life of Columbus. On the afternoon of the
second day Maria Huxley joined Frieda in his room. At 10
p. m. he died. He was laid to rest, with a simple ceremony,
in the hills of Vence. Ten people followed him on his final
journey. They buried him in the ground "like a dead bird,"
thought Frieda as she let the last flowers fall. Aldous
Huxley, who was with him to the end, writes in his introduction to Lawrence's *Letters*: "No headstone is over his
grave, save a phoenix (which was his own design), done
in local stone by a peasant who loved him."

The news of Lawrence's death was not reported in the
London press as fully or as respectfully as it should have

been. His sincere interest in the relationship between men and women had caused him to be misunderstood, so that neither the man nor his works could be discussed, for the time being, in "polite" society. Indeed, in *Journey With Genius,* Witter Bynner writes that "until almost a decade after his death the British Broadcasting Company would not allow his name to be mentioned."

Little by little the taboo was lifted. An anonymous writer in *The London Times Literary Supplement* declared:

Lawrence was the most remarkable and the most lovable man I have ever known. Contact with him was immediate, intimate, and rich. When he was gay, and he was often gay, . . . he seemed to spread a sensuous enchantment about him. By a natural magic he unsealed the eyes of all those in his company: birds and beasts and flowers became new-minted as in Paradise; they stood revealed as what they were, and not the poor objects of our dull and common seeing. The most ordinary domestic act—the roasting of a joint of meat, the washing up of crockery, the painting of a cottage room—in his doing became a . . . sacrament.

Catherine Carswell, insisting that Lawrence's life had been a spiritual victory, enumerated thus his various achievements:

In the face of . . . life-long delicacy, poverty that lasted for three-quarters of his life and hostility that survives his death, he did nothing that he did not really want to do, and all that he most wanted to do he did. He went all over the world, he owned a ranch, he lived in the most beautiful corners of Europe, and met whom he wanted to meet and told them that they were wrong and that he was right. He painted and made things and sang and rode. He wrote something like three dozen books, of which even the worst pages dance with life that could be mistaken for no other man's, while the best are admitted, even by those who hate him, to be unsurpassed.

Today, fortunately, there is no longer any need to insist on Lawrence's virtues as a writer or as a man. In spite of all his imperfections, something great shines through that commands respect. We understand now that he was struggling to express not only his own tensions, but the tensions of the age in which we live. And even though we may disagree with some of his opinions as to what is wrong with the world, and as to what is needed to put it right, we cannot escape being moved by what one critic has called "the expressional power of Lawrence's utterance." If, in other words, we think that we are not concerned with what he says, we are still very vitally concerned with how he says it. "His influence upon English fiction in the twentieth century," T. S. Eliot affirms, "has been as great as any of his contemporaries'."

BIBLIOGRAPHY

Aldington, Richard, D. H. Lawrence: *Portrait of a Genius, But*
... New York, Duell, Sloan and Pearce, 1950.

Brett, Dorothy, *Lawrence and Brett*. Philadelphia, J. B. Lippincott, 1933.

Brewster, Earl and Achsah, *Reminiscences of D. H. Lawrence*.
London, Martin Secker, 1934.

Bynner, Witter, *Journey with Genius: Recollections and Reflections Concerning the D. H. Lawrences*. New York, The John
Day Co., 1951.

Carswell, Catherine, *The Savage Pilgrimage*. New York, Harcourt, Brace and Co., 1932.

Gregory, Horace, *Pilgrim of the Apocalypse*. New York, The
Viking Press, 1933.

Kingsmill, Hugh, *The Life of D. H. Lawrence*. New York,
Dodge Publishing Co., 1938.

Lawrence, D. H., *Aaron's Rod*. New York, Thomas Seltzer, 1922.*

——, *Apocalypse*. (Introduction by Richard Aldington.) New
York, The Viking Press, 1932.

—— *Birds, Beasts and Flowers*. New York, Thomas Seltzer,
1923.*

—— *The Boy in the Bush* (In collaboration with M. L. Skinner.) New York, Thomas Seltzer, 1924.*

—— *Etruscan Places*. New York, The Viking Press, 1932.

—— *Kangaroo*. New York, Thomas Seltzer, 1923.*

—— *Lady Chatterley's Lover*. Florence, published by the
author, 1928.**

—— *Last Poems*. Florence, G. Orioli, 1932.*

—— *The Letters of D. H. Lawrence*. (Edited with introduction by Aldous Huxley.) New York, The Viking Press, 1932.

—— *The Lost Girl.* New York, Thomas Seltzer, 1921.*

—— *The Man Who Died.* New York, Alfred A. Knopf, Inc., 1931.

—— *Mornings in Mexico.* New York, Alfred A. Knopf, Inc., 1927.

—— *Phoenix: The Unpublished Papers of D. H. Lawrence.* New York, The Viking Press, 1936.

—— *The Plumed Serpent.* New York, Alfred A. Knopf, Inc., 1926.

—— *Sea and Sardinia.* New York, Thomas Seltzer, 1921.*

—— *St. Mawr.* New York, Alfred A. Knopf, Inc., 1925.

—— *The Woman Who Rode Away.* New York, Alfred A. Knopf, Inc., 1928.

Lawrence, Frieda, *Not I, But the Wind.* New York, The Viking Press, 1934.

Luhan, Mabel Dodge, *Lorenzo in Taos.* New York, Alfred A. Knopf, Inc., 1932.

Magnus, Maurice, *Memoirs of the Foreign Legion.* (Introduction by D. H. Lawrence.) New York, Alfred A. Knopf, Inc., 1925.

Merrild, Knud, *A Poet and Two Painters.* New York, The Viking Press, 1939.

Moore, Harry T., *The Life and Works of D. H. Lawrence.* New York, Twayne Publishers, 1951.

Murry, John Middleton, *Reminiscences of D. H. Lawrence.* New York, Henry Holt and Co., 1933.

—— *Son of Woman.* New York, Cape and Smith, 1931.

Nardi, Piero, *La Vita di D. H. Lawrence.* Milano, Mondadori, 1947.

Tiverton, Father William, *D. H. Lawrence and Human Existence.* (Foreword by T. S. Eliot.) New York, Philosophical Library, 1951.

West, Anthony, *D. H. Lawrence.* ("The English Novelists" Series.) London, Arthur Barker, 1950.

West, Rebecca, *D. H. Lawrence.* London, Martin Secker, 1930.

*Publishing rights in these titles are held by The Viking Press.
**Publishing rights in this title are held by Alfred A. Knopf, Inc.

INDEX

Index

Index

Index